# TRAIN
# FOR
# RESULTS

# TRAIN FOR RESULTS

**MAXIMIZE THE IMPACT OF
TRAINING THROUGH REVIEW**

## CATHERINE MATTISKE

TPC - The Performance Company Pty Ltd
PO Box 639
Rozelle NSW 2039
Sydney, Australia

ACN 077 455 273
email: info@tpc.net.au
Website: www.tpc.net.au

Published 2001 - Allen & Unwin
Published 2009 - TPC - The Performance Company Pty Limited

---

National Library of Australia
Cataloguing-in-Publication data

Mattiske, Catherine.
Train for results: maximize the impact of training through review.

Includes index
ISBN 978-1-921547-30-0

1. Occupational training. 2. Learning. I. Title.

370.113

---

Printed in USA

Distributed by TPC - The Performance Company - www.tpc.net.au
For further information contact TPC - The Performance Company, Sydney Australia
on +61 9555 1953 or TPC - The Performance Company, California on +1 818-227-5052,
or email info@tpc.net.au

*This book is dedicated*
*to my grandfather,*
*Harold Conrad Mattiske,*
*... a teacher of souls.*

# CONTENTS

# ABOUT THE AUTHOR

**CATHERINE MATTISKE** founded TPC - The Performance Company in 1994 and now has offices in Sydney Australia, New York, California and London. Catherine is a world-renowned leading training professional with over 2,500 days of face-to-face training experience since 1982. She has trained in both technical and non-technical training environments for leading organizations worldwide. Catherine Mattiske is a sought after speaker for conferences and training industry events. Catherine speaks at industry meetings such as ASTD, ISPI, ACRP and others. Catherine has trained across USA, Australia, Africa, Europe, New Zealand and Asia.

In 1998 Catherine Mattiske designed the breakthrough rapid instructional design methodology - ID9. The review activities in this book and the methods discussed form part of ID9. Catherine has certified thousands of corporate trainers in ID9 and as a result these trainers are reaping the rewards of saving time and money by using the ID9 system. Also, Catherine has written a series of Learning Short-takes on a variety of professional development topics. Each Learning Short-take is a training course in itself and able to be purchased via the TPC website.

Catherine's success as a trainer lies in her simple to follow, easy to retain training techniques. Catherine's success as consultant is due to ability to draw on years of training knowledge gained from every angle – upfront trainer, training manager, instructional designer and business owner. She has helped many companies across the globe change the way training is designed and delivered within their organizations.

Catherine Mattiske is considered a world authority on rapid instructional design that drives participant motivation, retention and application. Catherine writes training programs for many Fortune 100 organizations globally. She is able to instantly transform 'dull content' into 'dynamic training' – whatever the subject matter.

In 2003, 2005, 2006, and again in 2008, Catherine was nominated for the prestigious Australian Businesswomen of the Year. In June 2007, Catherine was appointed to the US Congressional Business Advisory Council - nominated by her clients for her influence to US business, and attended the President's Dinner in Washington DC.

# ACKNOWLEDGMENTS

I HAVE ALWAYS BELIEVED that 'anyone can write a book'. I still hold this belief. However, through the process of writing this book I have begun to learn the true meaning of synergy: the whole is greater than the sum of its parts. I wish to acknowledge and thank the following people for their part in the first print of this book in 2002 and this 2009 reprint.

For the first print of this book in 2002, I wish to again thank Michéle Malseed for her influence on my career as a trainer and for her role in the success of my business. I am also grateful to Michéle, a fellow training professional, for editing and commenting on drafts of this book.

To the many thousands of corporate trainers who have allowed me to explore the boundaries and possibilities of adult learning – thank you. I have always taught trainers that at the end of a training course it is the trainer who should have learned the most, thanks also to the 20,000 participants from whom I have had the opportunity to learn. It is the enthusiasm and dedication of both the trainers that I work with and the participants I teach that encourage me to continue to push the boundaries of my work as a professional trainer and instructional designer.

Lastly, for their personal encouragement during the time when I was writing this book my thanks goes to Tim Edwards and the B&P team, Andrea Rejante and Ian Bowring at Allen & Unwin, and in preparing for the 2009 reprint, Goran Rupena at Icarus Design.

With the help and encouragement of all of these people, I have begun the journey of learning about the true value and benefits of synergy. Thank you.

CATHERINE MATTISKE

# INTRODUCTION

In 2001, I was stopped in traffic on the Sydney Harbour Bridge, attempting to get home after a long day of training. It was a typical summer day in Sydney, humid and hot. The haze of car fumes enveloped the massive structure above me. Eight lanes of traffic had come to a halt. My survival strategy was straightforward enough. I had created a cocoon of air-conditioning and classical music. I then began to reflect on my exhausting training day.

I had just completed the first day of a three-day Train the Trainer course. I was thinking about a question that one of my participants asked me: 'Catherine, how long have you been training?' My immediate answer was 'since 1982' - the number of years I'd been training in a corporate environment. I realized that, in fact, there were three answers to that simple question: Since the 60's, Since 1982, and since 1998. These three answers began the journey of reflection on my life as an adult educator, trainer, presenter, facilitator and writer of training courses. The outcome of those three answers have now transpired to become this book. Let me explain.

I realized that I actually started training at in the 1960s. I set up my training room with my blackboard at the front and proceeded to train my very attentive participants in the issues of the day. I had been issued with two big boxes of chalk – the type only teachers used. One box was filled with smooth white chalk, the other was filled to capacity with at least ten different colors, making for very professional visual aids. My participants sat encouragingly in straight lines and seemed in awe of my lectures. At the end they whispered in my ear that it was the best training course they had ever been on and their lives had changed. I was just a child, in my sunlit bedroom with yellow wallpaper, teaching subjects like 'hosting afternoon tea parties' and 'learning the alphabet'. I completely wore out blackboards and my father was called on to repaint, repair and build me new, bigger, improved versions. I can't remember a time when I did not have a blackboard – it was truly my greatest childhood asset.

These days, I use flipchart paper and colored markers but, apart from the fact that my participants are real people, nothing much 'technologically' has changed. This is a paradox in itself. Despite having an early career in the computer training industry, I have resorted to flipchart paper and colored markers!

These days, it is my responsibility to ensure that at the end of a training course my participants are ready to apply what they have learned to their lives and work. Charged with this responsibility, I ensure that I have proved to myself and to each participant that they are ready. It is important for all trainers to realize that they are working with intelligent, competent people, and I always ensure that I treat participants as adults, not children.

My aim is to build a working relationship with each participant and allow them the freedom and safety to explore and develop their learning so that they can ultimately succeed. Words like 'coach', 'guide', 'help', 'care', 'responsibility', 'encouragement' and 'success' are of paramount importance to both me and the learner.

When I answered 'Since 1982' to the question, I was thinking about when I began training professionally. Like most professional trainers I meet, I fell into training, having been asked by my boss to train a new person joining our department. This was a very typical one-to-one unstructured training session. I had not prepared any notes, had no idea of which training approach would maximize his opportunity for success, nor had any time constraints or guidelines. My idea of training was to tell Roger everything I knew about the subject I was training regardless of whether it was relevant or not. When we chatted informally, I filled in the gaps that I had left out of my training. Somehow both Roger and I got through the experience.

My mark of success was that Roger survived and was able to cope with his job. My manager said I was good at teaching others and gave me several other opportunities to help new staff members. This made me reflect on what good training is all about. I resolved to focus on what participants needed to learn.

This book is dedicated to the learner being the centre of the training experience. The shift for you as a trainer is enormous, however the extra effort on your part is minimal. The results will speak for themselves and propel you to do more and more to make your training course their course not yours. This book will assist you to create activities that you can run during your training sessions that will help to avoid the ad hoc approach I used with Roger.

## THE AIM OF THIS BOOK

The aim of this book is to help you succeed in every training session you conduct. It will assist you to build activities to measure participants' learning. Then at the end of your training course you should be confident that your participants are ready to apply their learning to real situations.

Regardless of how many people you have trained or intend training, please keep reading! The benefit to you of adopting this new method is that you will maximize your potential success with each and every participant and that success will be reflected, without effort, back to you.

With persistence, patience and an open mind, you will get that bit closer to the ultimate trainer's goal: guaranteed 100% success with 100% of participants 100% of the time. And, when you get there you have created a miracle that no one else has ever created!

## TECHNICAL TRAINING

My knowledge and experience as a trainer went on to be forged in the domain of computer training. In the early 1980s, with the advent of PCs, I found myself training a group of six participants in word processing. I had written a 300-page reference manual to replace the 100-page reference manual that came with the computer! My participants and I ploughed through the system, learning by a series of exercises and hands-on activities. A technical person who had no experience of adult learning touted the training as a great success!

Unfortunately, I still see this 'reference manual approach' to technical training. Often technical trainers focus so heavily on the technical side of their work they forget (consciously or unconsciously) that there is learning involved. In technical training the learner can and must be the centre of the training experience. With a shift in focus, technical trainers can also employ the methods described in this book. If you are a technical trainer working in any computer related or process-related field you will benefit greatly from including review activities in your training sessions. You will learn that by including these activities, your participants will be more confident with their new system and will advance at a much faster pace than before.

## MAKING LEARNING ENJOYABLE

From the mid-80s to the early 90's, I conducted lots of face-to-face training, and I rejected totally the idea that training had to be boring, difficult and dry. I felt that participants should expect to succeed and to be able to confidently apply their learnings back at their workplace. To that end, I considered such things as room layout, catering, training materials, training activities, and the quality of the trainers hired to do the job.

When I started my own business in 1994, I took these ideas and developed them. Now I take these same ideas to broader business with broader training requirements — not just with technical training but all training. The one thing that was of paramount importance was to **put the learner at the centre of the training experience**. Training programs should be designed for learners, taking into account their skill level, and delivered by professional trainers who speak their language and can demystify technology in an environment that is safe, friendly and where 'test-driving' and making mistakes is encouraged.

Part of the mix of things we did back then was to make review activities part of each session. Participants built their confidence because they were showing themselves that they were progressing. They were bolstered through the experience with a 'we can do it' approach, rather than a traditional 'this is going to be tough' approach. On reflection, this took hardly any time at all, but was a tremendous pay-off for all involved.

A trainer I was working with commented: 'Think of training like a pie — all the different aspects of what we do are slices. The room layout, the music, the way we approach training, the variety of adult learning styles that we cater for, the lack of jargon, the colored flipcharts, PowerPoint slideshows, the review activities — they're all slices. When it comes to impact and long-term gain , it's the slice called "review activities" that is the one that makes the difference. It is so huge that without it, everything else just seems like nice things to have. If we took out reviews, the training may still be good, but not necessarily last long-term.'

Review activities are just a slice in the overall 'success pie'. All of the slices contribute to a participant being central to the training focus. Review activities are put into courses for both the trainer and the participant. Trainers know that their participants are on track and learning. Participants increase their confidence, knowing that they are 'getting it' and can fill any gaps in their learning as they happen or soon after, without steering too much off track.

## EXPLORING MY PERSONAL STYLE

The third possible answer to how long I'd been training was 'Since 1998'. Why do I say this? I started my consultancy business in 1994, taking time out from being a manager and working as a contract trainer for many different organizations. This allowed me to explore and push the boundaries of my personal training style. I knew that I could walk into any training course, and deliver a great course; participants said they loved my courses and felt they were having fun. I never considered having fun as important and still don't — it's nice if they do have fun, but learning is often difficult and hard work. The critical thing is whether participants have learned what I set out to teach them, (the learning objectives) and whether they can apply that learning to their work.

### SENSATIONAL EVALUATIONS — MY BIGGEST PROBLEM!

At that time, I was training five days every week. I was booked months in advance, and I was getting sensational evaluations. And that was the problem. I was motivated purely by the spotlight of training, the cash-in-bank advantages and the accolades from participants and senior managers. I can honestly say that I had neither care nor responsibility for the learning that took place in my room, just the end result, which was to keep myself in the business of training. I took stock of my style and of what I should truly be aiming for.

# IT'S NOT YOUR COURSE — IT'S THEIR COURSE

My most important belief became, and remains: **it's not your course — it's their course**. It's not the trainers course, it's the participants course. When I train professional trainers and say this to them, usually the response is quite flippant. 'Oh yes,' they say, 'of course, it's their course.' But to take this notion seriously is a huge step as a trainer, perhaps one of the most important steps a trainer will take, if they take it at all.

It means that you must have all care and all responsibility to ensure your participants are fully equipped and ready to apply their learning to their workplace the moment each participant leaves your training program. It means that you must, as their trainer, build their confidence to ensure that they are open to working outside their comfort zone. You should support them when they succeed and more importantly when they don't. It means that you must collect hard and soft data to support your claim that they indeed can apply what you have taught them (whether internally voiced to yourself or externally voiced to others). It means that you may have to fight the bureaucracy and norms of your own corporate training environment that have been in place for decades and convince, or at least persuade others, that your ideas have merit.

## WHAT DOES THIS MEAN FOR THE TRAINER?

In my experience, when a professional trainer takes this step, they will have one of two possible responses. The first response comes from the weaker trainer, who might give up and might even leave training forever because the notion of 'it's their course' is too hard to deal with. They choose not to invest in the thought it requires, the preparation, effort and energy required to convince others that this approach has merit. Even though they know that the possibility of outstanding success exists at the other end they give up. To know that a new dimension of training exists and not adopt the new method is sometimes considered as personal failure. Often this feeling comes, not from others, but from themselves. If they had tried and experimented with this new dimension of training, they would have realized how easy the process really is, however complex it may have looked at first glance.

The second response comes from the professional trainer, who will persist, reflect and re-evaluate what they have been doing in their training. Over time such re-evaluation will result in an outstanding metamorphosis as to who they are as a trainer. It also radically changes the results that they get. They may have received sensational evaluation forms before this radical departure from their old ways. However, using this new strategy the professional trainer will find that they never again need to seek out accolades or 'blow their own trumpet'. This is because the success they foster before, during and after their training comes back to them tenfold. The accolades will come to the trainer without their pushing or prodding. Every evaluation will be sensational, senior people will delight in having their staff well skilled and the personal demand for the trainer will look after itself, regardless of their internal of external position or capacity.

The professional trainer will look and strive for the success of others and will be re-fuelled again and again to recreate this success every time they train, so success will be theirs. The professional trainer knows that only minor adjustments need to be made. Therein lies the paradox. A minor adjustment of focus, like a slight shift of a compass on a map, will lead you to a totally new place.

## WHAT IS THE PROCESS TO BEGIN THE CHANGE IN APPROACH?

One of the ways to effectively put this new approach of responsibility and accountability into place is the process of 'reviews' — the process of ensuring that all participants show you and themselves that they know and can apply the material they have learned. It is not the only thing that makes successful training. However, from the words of one trainer who uses reviews: 'It takes up so much of the success pie. To leave it out is to question why you would bother going in to your training room!'

## COMPARING REVIEWS WITH OTHER 'TRAINING TECHNIQUES'

Reviews should not be compared with training games and they are not a technique to add 'fun' or gimmicks to training. A training game can be used successfully or not, for many purposes — as an icebreaker, to connect participants, to introduce material, to explore learning in more depth, to distance or approach material, to make a point or sometimes (unfortunately) just for 'fun'.

Review activities focus only on material already taught and they are run at various intervals during the training course.

# DEFINING REVIEW ACTIVITIES

A review activity is a way of measuring skills and knowledge during the running of the training course. It reassures participants that they are learning. It reassures trainers that they are successfully transferring skills and knowledge.

In Chapter 1 this definition is explored and discussed in depth. For now, it is appropriate to move across the surface of this large topic.

## A TRAINING TECHNIQUE VERSUS A CONTINUAL PROCESS

The process of reviewing material learned throughout a training course is measured inside the training room. A review activity is conducted at least six times in each training day to check understanding and combat gaps and questions that bubble to the top. To evaluate the potential success of each participant is not a technique, it is a continual process that requires the trainer to be dedicated to his or her ultimate goal., That is, to care for and share in the responsibility of the success of each participant.

This process is outlined in the chapters ahead and provide clear directions on what to do, and when, where and how to maximize your chances of success.

## IF REVIEWS ARE IN, THEN WHAT'S OUT?

I think of training courses like intricate structures — buildings of intertwined concepts and processes. Reviews do not take the place of any other training 'technique', rather they are added to the structure, like support beams in a building. They can be added into existing courses and your existing style and delivery technique. A new trainer can also quickly adopt this process and in doing so will be ahead of many of his or her seasoned colleagues. Amazingly, review activities do not require any further training time; they allow you to change the pace of your training to accommodate them. They can even save you training time, a paradox which I will detail later.

Regardless of whether you are a new trainer with a single storey building of training experience, or like me with a skyscraper of training experience, you can successfully build on this process to create a new dimension of brilliance to every training course that you conduct.

## CHANGING A MINDSET

Going back to the question how long had I been training, I thought about what has made me successful as a trainer. It is not more than 2,000 days of training I have conducted since 1982. It is not the 20,000 participants that have 'gone through' my training courses. It is that I changed my thinking since 1998. So the answer that I should have given should have 'since 1998'.

Five years before and for many before that, I truly thought many participants were lesser to me because they didn't have the skills and knowledge that I did. I thought of some as even downright horrible, others provocative, rude, dramatic, complaining, attacking, whining, moaning and groaning, and a few whom, in my opinion, were miserable people experiencing miserable lives. Many times they annoyed me, made my life difficult, made me stressed, and I openly complained about them behind their backs, to other like-minded trainers. Together the trainers would huddle on breaks and do our own fair share of moaning and groaning, although in front of these participants, we wore masks of friendliness and professionalism.

Now, since I've acknowledged that the largest slice of the success pie is ensuring that participants have retained their new skills and knowledge, have ability and can apply their learning, and recognized my responsibilities as a trainer, I do not have these sorts of 'lesser' participants. My participants know that I share in the responsibility of their learning. They know this because they can see the amount of preparation I put into their course. They know this because of the amount of pre-work I do with them before they arrive on the training day. Together we travel through the training course to meet their goals. Then, after the course, in consultation with their Manager, the participant and I ensure that the learning is applied.

Through the review process they show me, and more importantly themselves, that they know. They show themselves that they can do it, and can then apply their learning to their workplace. In the words of social psychologist Robert Cialdini, 'People are more likely to be consistent with their behavior, if they have openly committed to it'. They prove to themselves and show others that they are learning, progressing and becoming increasingly confident and when they do this, they don't get wrapped up in schoolyard antics. They treat me with the respect of a coach and guide who is clearly on the same side as them rather than resorting to treating me like a lecturing teacher.

## GETTING TO THE POINT

This was what I was thinking that day in my car as I was stopped on the Sydney Harbour Bridge. The question that I posed to myself was — how many of the 20,000 participants who I have trained have actually learned and been ready to apply their learning when they returned from my training course to their workplace? I will never know. But I know that since 1998, when my participants have left my training course they are ready. Before the training when I am writing, during the training when I am training, and after the training when I am conducting post-course work, I frequently ask myself this one basic question: **how do I know they know**? If I can answer this question at the end of each and every training program, I am on track to achieving success.

### THE DILEMMA OF MEASURING TRAINING

As most adult educators know, measuring what participants know cannot be done at a single point in time. The application of the learning needs to be measured before, during and after the training program has been conducted. It is this very point which prompted me to write this book on the 'during' part of the measurement equation. **My question to you is: 'When they leave your training course, do you know they know?'**

## USING THIS BOOK

So that you can fully understand the foundation concepts of building, running and debriefing review activities, as well as the placement of the review activities within the day, I would recommend that you read, rather than skim, Chapters 1–4. After reading these chapters, you may choose to use this book as an on-going reference to glean ideas and use the review activities that are included. In my experience, trainers use this material in an on-going way when writing new training courses or revamping existing training courses.

## AN OVERVIEW OF THE STRUCTURE OF THIS BOOK

Chapters 1, 2 and 3 cover definitions and the necessary foundation material needed to set up a successful training framework. In these chapters, I explore the benefits to participants, trainers and the organization, of running review activities within your training. The placement of pre-course in relationship with conducting review activities during the course is discussed at length. Many trainers currently measure training before and after the training intervention. However, as review activities measure learning during the training, it is vital to see the correlation and link of the three different styles of training measures. In Chapter 3, I have explored four popular myths associated with measuring learning. This is to give professional trainers a springboard for further discussion and research, which perhaps will eventually change the practice of training.

Chapters 4, 5 and 6 are about getting ready to create review activities, and discuss the decisions that trainers need to make when creating a training course, including the choice of review activities that will ultimately become a part of the course. Making the right decisions on content style, goals, level of participation and individual needs, will maximize the chances of greater success during and after the training. To assist in this process of decision making, I have provided explanations of training styles, how to link review activities to the training course goals, and how to match the needs of adult learners to the review process.

When to review is covered in Chapter 7, where I have provided the structure I use for half-day, one day, two day, three day and multi-day courses. You can use these templates to help place review activities in balance with other content. I have also suggested types of reviews that meet individual learning needs. You may photocopy these and use these templates for your own use in course development. I also look at the role of the trainer during the review.

Chapter 8 is a reference library of review activities that have worked for both myself and many other trainers. Each review activity has been conducted on countless numbers of participants in a variety of technical and non-technical training courses. Step-by-step instructions will guide you to make the review activity, conduct it, and most importantly debrief the learnings from it.

Chapter 9 examines some debriefing strategies. If you have time to carefully read only a couple of chapters of this book, then Chapters 7, 8 and 9 are the ones I would recommend. You will learn how to establish gaps in learning as a result of the review and know how to fill these gaps without taking your training off course. I have also specifically focused on the essential elements of debriefing that specifically relate to review activities, and have provided sample debrief questions.

In Chapter 10, I discuss some tips and tricks to assist you. This chapter is like a Pandora's box of ways to bring together ideas, save time and save money. It contains tips that I have collected over my years of training. They might not conquer all your training issues, but they will make your corporate training life a little easier.

Enjoy!

# CHAPTER ONE

# REVIEW ACTIVITIES DEFINED

* WHAT DOES A REVIEW ACTIVITY DO?

* 'TRAINING ACTIVITY' VERSUS 'REVIEW ACTIVITY'

* HANDLING KNOWLEDGE GAPS

A review activity is conducted during the training course to measure skills and knowledge. A review activity reassures participants that they are learning, and it reassures trainers that they are successfully transferring skills and knowledge.

## WHAT DOES A REVIEW ACTIVITY DO?

A review activity checks and measures the learning on a particular topic or group of topics while the participants are still in the training room. For example, in an Introduction to Windows training course, a review activity might be conducted immediately after participants have learnt the parts of the desktop and the parts of a window. This topic might include the scroll bar, title bar, menus and toolbars. The review may take the form of a fill-in-the-blanks puzzle, where the trainer draws up a flip chart with a giant screen capture of a window on it or, easier still, prints it on a plotter. Participants are given stick-on flags, each flag labelled with a part of the window, and they place their flags onto the flip chart pointing to the corresponding parts of the window. When all parts are identified, the trainer goes through each part and, with the group, checks for accuracy, asking in-depth questions along the way. The completed picture is posted on the training wall for the rest of the course as a prompt. This example is a group activity, but it could easily be done as an individual exercise with a handout.

In this example, the whole process may take as little as five minutes; however, the benefit for the trainer is twofold. First, the trainer knows that the participants know the correct terminology. Second, for the rest of the course the trainer can confidently tell people to 'Click on minimise — great'. If participants aren't familiar with this most basic of basic terminology, the trainer gets led down the disastrous path of saying things like, 'Click on minimise, no not that one. Now click here, here, here, okay, you're back to where you were — [sigh] — now click minimise. It's the button with the little line in the top right corner of the screen. That's it, good.' I used to find myself in situations where I sounded more like a broken record than a trainer!

This second benefit saves you loads of frustration and ensures that the whole group is kept travelling at a much more even pace throughout the day, not to mention the huge time saving entailed by being able to give instructions once! So, for a five-minute investment in the review activity, the benefits are endless — for both them and you!

## WHAT IS THE PURPOSE OF THE REVIEW ACTIVITY?

The purpose of a review activity is to ensure that you are meeting clearly established training goals and objectives. The choice and placement of the review are relatively straightforward. A trap for trainers who are starting out adding reviews to their courses is that sometimes 'the point' of the review gets muddied by the desire to produce exciting activities that not only enhance learning but breathe life into the course.

In order to be truly successful and a true measure of learning, the review activity must have a set outcome for participants. If the standard (or goal) is not set then how will you know when your participants have met it?

## A FOUNDATION STEP: WRITING YOUR COURSE GOAL

Like so many aspects of training, you get from it what you put into it. This applies to both trainers and participants. Trainers who 'wing it' run the risk not only of participants realising that they are ill-prepared, thus destroying their credibility and weakening their message, but also of wasting time. You need to focus if you want greater capacity to tap into learning opportunities.

Before preparing individual review activities, be sure you have an overall course goal. Investing just a few minutes of preparation time in setting objectives for the entire course will plot your path for what you expect from your participants. It will help if you write your course goal and objective clearly in your training materials. While preparing your course, ensure that all activities and content support your goal. If something does not fully and completely serve and support your goal, remove it or rewrite it. Put your goal on a flip chart during the welcome phase of your training course. When you've formulated your course goal, ask: 'When they leave my training course, how will I know that they know?'

# WHAT TOPICS ARE INCLUDED?

The topics that are reviewed might range from conceptual to step-by-step process information. For example, in a customer service training course you can review the concepts of getting to know your customers, accepting personal responsibility and valuing difficult customers as effectively as entering customer details into the company database or the seven steps to good customer service.

For the concept-type topics, the customer service trainer might choose to do a simple 'statement and question' review activity. Statements pertaining to the training topics and questions about each statement are prepared on cards. Participants work in pairs or small groups and draw, from the stack of question cards, five cards per team. For the topic of 'Check for Understanding' an example might be: 'Understand what your customer is saying by checking to make sure. Repeat back to the customer what you think you heard and see if you are correct. When are important times for you to check for understanding?' Teams answer the question and share their responses with the entire training group. When debriefing this review, the trainer can engage the entire group to increase the depth of learning. By asking more questions about each card, the trainer can help to identify any gaps and enhance the learning of the whole group.

For step-by-step topics, a trainer might choose an equally simple step mix. The steps to the process are written on individual cards and these are shuffled. Participants put them in order and check that they are correct. This activity can be made more difficult by jumbling several step-by-step processes in the one stack. Participants need to separate them into the different processes, then put each process in order. The trainer can debrief this review with a 'what-if' line of questioning: 'What if I swapped these two steps? What if I left this step out? What if I added x here? What if I skipped this whole section? What if I did this process in the middle of the day and not at the end of the day? What would happen if I left this process for others to do?'

## 'TRAINING ACTIVITY' VERSUS 'REVIEW ACTIVITY'

Training activities are usually conducted immediately after the trainer gives theoretical or practical information. During the activity learning is still taking place. It might be the first time that participants get to try out their new skills or learning. During training activities the participant is usually doing a fully scripted and guided exercise. In a review activity, skills and knowledge are measured during the training course, reassuring participants that they are learning, and trainers that they are successfully transferring skills and knowledge.

### A WORKING EXAMPLE: PERFORMANCE IMPROVEMENT

You are training a course in performance improvement for managers and supervisors, specifically in the area of identifying problems and giving feedback. Let's explore how regular training activities, training content and review activities work together to create a situation where the trainer knows the message has been successfully delivered.

After the topic is introduced, you conduct a training activity in which participants list problems they have had in the workplace where they felt feedback was necessary. You then address some ways of giving feedback to staff using a model of effective feedback. The model has been documented as the standard way managers give feedback within the organisation. You demonstrate the model with an example of how it works in practice.

You conduct another training activity where participants are given two situations, namely 'Bob is always late' and 'Sally frequently carries on aside conversations during meetings'. Participants are given a range of questions to answer, such as what's the problem, why is this a problem, whose problem is it, what are the possible consequences of the situation, and what should be done, when, where, how and by whom? Participants answer as part of a whole group activity. Up to now 'training activities' have taken place.

As a review activity you choose to do a 'pick a card' review in small groups. You have prepared 20 problem situations. Each group draws five cards and uses the model and the sample questions to create a solution on giving feedback for each situation. They share their solutions with the whole group. The trainer then debriefs the review activity, ensuring that all participants know the model and can apply the model in their day-to-day working life. In this example, the review activity is added to ensure that the participants know and can apply their learning to real-life situations. During the regular training activities, the participants were still learning — they were not consolidating their learning.

## HOW MANY PARTICIPANTS ARE INVOLVED IN A REVIEW ACTIVITY?

Review activities can be designed for individual participants, pairs, small groups or large groups. I have run review activities with one participant as effectively as with a group of 700 participants. A mix of different review activities provides variety for the participants and the trainer and, more important, different levels of participation help to support and provide for people's different learning styles. A mix of whole-group, team-based, pair-and-share, individual and metacognitive (or reflective) reviews should be in every training course, regardless of duration or participant job title and experience.

## WHAT FORM DOES A REVIEW ACTIVITY TAKE?

The review activity may be a handout, a card sort, a puzzle, a board game or a competition.

Some will take little or no preparation, while others will require more lead time. A review activity may be as simple as 'squad challenge', where the trainer asks participants in small groups to write down questions to ask an opposing team of participants. This takes no preparation time on the trainer's part, but is an excellent way to review the content both for the questioning team and the answering team. The questioning team is reviewing the content when composing questions; the answering team is reviewing content by coming up with the answers.

An example of a review activity requiring preparation is a board game. Many commercially available games have boards that can easily be adapted for a training review. You need to write the questions, know the rules clearly and be able to facilitate the game or create your own. Preparation may take 30 minutes or several hours, but once the game is made, it can be used time and time again, making it a wise investment of preparation time.

## HOW MUCH TIME DOES A REVIEW ACTIVITY TAKE TO RUN?

A review activity may be conducted for five minutes or two hours. The duration depends on how much material is being reviewed, and the nature of the success criteria. A simple step mix where participants put into order the steps of a sequence might take only a few minutes to conduct and debrief. I use these types of quick-to-run review activities in my training courses up to 10 to 15 times a day. Many of these aren't even identified by participants as review activities — they do them without any announcement or fanfare!

Other more complex reviews, for example a start-of-day review that covers the topics from the previous day, might take up to 90 minutes. In an advanced course called Train the Trainer Master Class, I conduct a review on the morning of the second day that involves a jigsaw puzzle (showing a course design process taught on the previous day), story writing and presentation techniques. This reviews content from the previous day, as well as being a springboard for more in-depth content later in the course.

During this review, participants are unwittingly sitting a 90 minute exam; however, at no time do they feel they are being tested or examined. If people thought they were sitting an exam, they probably wouldn't be happy! And when you take into account nerves and tension, results can be muddied and fail to give me a real indication of what they know. At the end of this review activity I know that they know and, if they don't, I have an opportunity to fill gaps before moving on to more content.

A review activity is not designed to be fun. If fun happens then it might make the review activity more memorable. Many review activities create a sense of fun and enjoyment. One of my favourites is Money Bags. Based on the popular U.S. television program Jeopardy, opposing teams compete furiously for points by answering prepared questions on a particular category. 'Money' is awarded for correct answers, and the team with the most 'money' wins. Each time I conduct Money Bags, which is simply a disguised test of 16 questions, I know that the by-product of the review process will be outrageous competition, laughter and fun. Regardless of my participants' job descriptions within their organisation, the outcome is always intense battle to answer questions correctly. If you have never conducted Money Bags before, try it. There are instructions in Chapter 8. All fun aside, Money Bags is an excellent review activity that fully engages participants in reviewing content. And that's the point — fun is great in any training course, but make sure that your review activity actually reviews content. You should also ensure that the review activity uses time well. An activity that takes 30 minutes and reviews only two or three minor points is worthless.

### WHAT HAPPENS AFTER THE REVIEW ACTIVITY?

After the review activity, participants should be debriefed. Here, the trainer explores further questions, comments and fills knowledge gaps of individual participants. As a rule of thumb, the debrief should take about half of the activity time. For example, a true/false review should take ten minutes. To debrief the review well, which includes checking the results, asking further questions and clarifying issues, you could expect to take at least a further five minutes. This is an extremely important task. Chapter 9 provides step-by-step instructions for designing and conducting a successful debrief.

## HOW DO I HANDLE KNOWLEDGE GAPS?

As I have mentioned, during the debrief stage, the trainer is actively searching for gaps in participants' knowledge or understanding. Most gaps identified in a review activity can be filled there and then as part of the debrief process. For example, a misunderstood definition, a concept requiring clarification or a poorly ordered step sequence can quickly be seen to during the debrief.

## WHAT ABOUT BIG GAPS?

When a large gap is identified that can't be remedied quickly, there are two facts that must be unearthed: first, how many of your participants are affected and, second, what is the effect?

Where a whole group is affected, then my approach is not to continue with new material until the gap is filled. If you continue without filling the gap, you run the risk of creating more confusion. And, anyway, it's often impossible for them to move on. This is because the gap in their knowledge and the confusion are openly discussed and participants realise that they are not alone with the problem. If you let this opportunity go then you'll have to revisit the problem later in the course. So fix it now.

There is one exception to this approach. Say you are the trainer of a Microsoft Word training course and during a post-lunch review activity a problem with setting tabs is identified. You taught tabs first thing that day and went on well past the time allocated to this topic. Some equipment problems mean that you are further behind time. The topic of creating tables is coming up later that afternoon, with one of the subtopics being 'converting tabbed text to a table'. This is what I call a 'hanging issue'. A good strategy would be to explain to the group that when we do tables, instead of opening a pre-existing file that uses tabs (ready for them to convert to a table), we will create our own tabbed list and in the process review setting tabs. To lend certainty to this change in direction (and so that you remember to do it), write 'review setting tabs' on a 'Hanging Issues' flip chart on the training room wall. This saves time because you are 'bolting' the gap filler onto another topic. A key skill of any professional trainer is flexibility and, if you know your content before you walk into your training room, changes can be made swiftly and confidently for the benefit of both your participants and you, the trainer.

When a small group of participants has a knowledge gap, a further question should be asked: 'What is the result of these people missing this knowledge?' The answer for most corporate trainers working with strained budgets and time constraints is that it has significant impact, for little the corporate trainer does these days is padding or unimportant content. Traditionally, the approach might have been to spend time filling the gap with the participants concerned and hold up the others. This punishes everyone. Those with the gap feel guilty for holding up the rest of the group; the others feel punished because they are made to wait for the stragglers. With a slight twist, this problem can present a real opportunity for a skilled trainer.

One option might be to engage a cooperative learning strategy whereby your create pairs of participants — one with the gap, the other with the knowledge. The skilled person takes on a teaching role to bring the other up to speed; the unskilled participant gains a private coach. The skilled participant solidifies their knowledge by teaching someone else. A second option might be to split your group for a short time during the training course. You can dedicate this time to the unskilled group. The skilled group can be given more advanced work in the same topic area, an extra activity to stretch their knowledge or a further review activity on the same or a different topic. You should not make them wait or give them 'busy work'. Don't waste an opportunity to use training time for valuable learning.

This issue is raised in almost every training course a skilled professional trains. As you become more adept at conducting reviews, so too will your 'gap filling' strategies improve. As an easy start, I suggest that you prepare extra review activities and numerous practical activities and handouts as contingency measures.

Remember that participants who have identified themselves as having a gap in their knowledge may feel exposed. It is your job to remedy the situation quickly while maintaining a positive state of mind. The psychological effect of having a confident prepared trainer, who can simply go to 'plan B' to help them to move on, rather than a flustered unprepared trainer could mean the well-being of the participant is not diminished.

Where only one participant is affected, you can usually remedy the situation quickly and simply. If regular review activities are being conducted throughout the day, the little problems that bubble to the surface can be fixed without too much fuss. At other times, fixing the problem of an individual participant is a delicate operation in which you risk exposing the participant and making them feel stupid, losing the momentum of the group's learning and losing patience.

The techniques discussed above for filling gaps for small groups may be your first approach. Using cooperative learning is often a great way to get results. However, sometimes the participant taking the training role loses momentum, feeling held up by the process. If a trainer continues with the cooperative learning strategy beyond that time, the participant in the training role will become frustrated and resentful.

Analyse why the individual concerned is not at the same level as the rest of the group. Find out the participant's intended application for the learning. In training courses I have conducted I have had this very difficulty. The course was an Advanced Excel course, covering spreadsheet complexities like pivot tables, macros and advanced formulas. Reviews were paramount. One participant, Jane, struggled through the first day of the two-day course. There was no time to do major backtracking. Jane was fine until the advanced formula section. That section's review activity was an individual review where participants matched the question with its answer. There were five extra answers that made it more difficult than a mere guessing game. During the review activity, I found that Jane's depth of knowledge was inadequate. She had kept up through guided activities but did not do very well on her own. Because of the safe learning environment that had been created, Jane decided to do some more on this section alone, choosing to miss the next session on macros because she felt that macros were not as important for her purposes as advanced formulas. She made the call, not me. I gave her some extra activities on advanced formulas, which I had prepared as a contingency measure, and she was happy to work alone seeking my help at opportune moments. When she redid the review activity she was delighted with her results.

It is important that known gaps in knowledge be flagged and recorded by the trainer as part of a post-course training administration system so that after the course these gaps can be filled or, at the very least, planned for.

Whatever the subject matter, this approach works. From project management to safety training, allowing participants to make their own decisions about their learning — in consultation with you — gives them ownership of their learning.

# SOME PRE-COURSE MEASURES TO CONSIDER

Even though the focus of this book is measuring learning during the training, I'd like to focus briefly on the 'before' part of the measuring process to put things in context.

## BEFORE TRAINING: PRE-COURSE MEASURES

Sometimes I see evidence that trainers are conducting good pre-course measures. However, this pre-course work is rarely excellent. When I began my own business, I would cruise into the training company at 8.30 a.m. ready to start my course at 9.00 a.m. I'd peruse the list detailing the participants' names and their organisations. At 9.00 a.m. sharp the trainers would announce their courses, and my participants would follow me dutifully to the training room. Until that time, we had never met — they were just names on a piece of paper. It took a lot of valuable training time to establish, among other things, why they were doing the course, their existing skill level, what they needed the skills for, and to build rapport with them. Even though this method annoyed and frustrated me, I thought I had no choice. As a contract trainer I could not contact them before the course. I didn't have that information and couldn't get it. The challenge was to find some way of connecting with my participants prior to the course. The solution was simple.

Instead of arriving at 8.30 a.m. I arrived at 8.00 a.m. I set up my training room and then, with 30 to 40 minutes to spare, searched out my participants and introduced myself. We chatted over coffee. This had so many advantages. The participants relaxed and so did I. Because it was informal, they discussed their needs and objectives openly. They connected with the course, each other and me. The result was that they were no longer names on a list, but real people with real needs. It made my job as a trainer much simpler. At the beginning of the course, I could quickly convert our informal chat into a formal list of needs. This got the course off to a positive start and freed up more time for me to concentrate on participants' learning.

Another benefit for me was that I had very few surprises when I got into the training room. All trainers can take this simple step. These days I have full control over the amount of pre-course work that I do with my participants. I do pre-course questionnaires, information sheets, send the participants a course outline, the logistics of locations, plus a pack to their manager telling them what our training goals are and what their role in the process is. It makes for a very smooth-running course.

My aim is to maximise the impact of the training session — so the more work I do prior to the course, the more impact my training has. Time spent prior to the course is time saved during the course. This saved time is used to conduct review activities and provide extra content. There is no doubt that there is an increasing trend to conduct pre-course work, either as a questionnaire (to learn about participants' current roles and course objectives) or pre-course activities (such as reading textbooks).

Yet there are still many trainers who know little or nothing about their participants' work and prior learning before the course starts. Why don't they want to know? Why don't they want a better rapport with participants? How can they structure their course when they don't know where to pitch the material? Why don't they want to save time? The questions go on!

The link between pre-course work and review activities is of paramount importance. Chapter 8 shows you how to design review activities that establish how much knowledge your participants have when they get into the training room and how to create review activities to build on that knowledge. However, in order to design these activities for maximum impact, you need to have employed some sort of pre-course work strategy so that neither you nor your participants are flying blind. For your own sake, conduct some form of pre-course work. Once you try it you'll never look back!

## SUMMARY

A review activity measures skills and knowledge during the training course. It reassures participants that they are learning. It reassures trainers that they are successfully transferring skills and knowledge. It is conducted while the participants are still in the training room. The topics that are reviewed can range from conceptual to step-by-step process information.

In order to be truly successful and a true measure of learning, the review activity must have a set outcome for participants.

Review activities can be designed for individual participants, pairs or small or large groups. They can consist of a handout, a card sort, a puzzle, a board game or a competition.

They can take five minutes or two hours, depending on how much material is being reviewed and the nature of the success criteria.

While review activities are not designed to be fun, if they are this can make the review activity more memorable. Following the review activity, the trainer conducts a debriefing, in which further questions, comments and knowledge gaps of individual participants are fully explored.

# CHAPTER TWO

# WHO BENEFITS FROM REVIEW ACTIVITIES?

* BENEFIT TO THE PARTICIPANT

* BENEFIT TO THE TRAINER

* BENEFIT TO THE ORGANISATION

# WHAT IS THE BENEFIT?

The review activity forms the bridge between learning the course content and applying that content in the workplace. It's the first step in the transfer of learning from the training room to the workplace. How does the bridge work?

**FIGURE 2.1** // BRIDGE BETWEEN TRAINING CONTENT AND WORKPLACE APPLICATION

THE REVIEW LINKS CONTENT TO APPLICATION

Conducting review activities as a measure during the course benefits:
- the participant
- the trainer
- the organisation (either the participant's organisation, or the trainer's organisation if the trainer is external).

# BENEFIT TO THE PARTICIPANT

Conducting review activities on a regular basis throughout the training day consolidates participants' knowledge. Completing a review activity, being part of a team in a highly competitive activity and participating in group activities all contribute to self-esteem and confidence. Participants also benefit from individual review activities, by working independently and reflecting, and from doing review activities with a partner (pair-and-share activities).

## PARTICIPANTS GAIN CONFIDENCE

By knowing the answers, participants show themselves and others that they can do it. For many participants learning is tough; hard work and conscientiousness are needed if they are to apply what they have learnt. Over the years, many of my participants have commented: 'I'll practise back at work' or 'I'll look over it again later when I have time'. Their lives as busy professionals often get in the way of their good intentions. From the most senior professional to the newest recruit in any organisation, participants need to feel confident throughout the entire training course.

Scheduling review activities helps maintain their level of confidence and keeps the pace of learning brisk. If participants lose confidence in their ability to master the material, the rate of learning declines, not only for themselves but also for the trainer.

## PARTICIPANTS REFUEL AND ARE READY FOR MORE CONTENT

Participants refuel when they are given a structured break from taking in new information. It's different from a coffee break where you can choose to 'switch off' from the training experience. During the review activity, participants are breaking from having to learn new content, while concentrating on the ground they have covered. This break in pace, together with the positive result from the review activity, gives them the drive to continue.

During a training course, participants are consciously and unconsciously doing many things at once. Most participants competently listen to the trainer, take notes, think about how they might apply what they are learning and how they will remember the important points. Of course, they are also thinking about their lives outside the training room — what's happening back at work, at home, what will they cook for dinner and endless other matters. With all this brain activity, is it any wonder participants are tired by the end of the training day?

A review activity is like group parallel thinking (a term used by Edward de Bono with reference to his six thinking hats concept). For a period of time, the whole group is thinking in a similar vein. They may be focusing on how to apply their learning, finding the answers to solve a quiz, putting conceptual content into action or simply putting process steps into the correct sequence. In other words, during a review activity the endless range of thought processes is narrowed down to a focused activity. This phenomenon happens without the trainer really doing anything more than facilitating the review activity. These refuelling stops during a course become times when participants can stop taking in new content and process the content they have already learnt. Many trainers would argue that, unless participants are given these 'refuelling stops' in the guise of review activities, not much actual learning takes place at all.

Refuelling rebuilds energy, drive and confidence. Participants need to be able to say to themselves: 'I've got it', 'I see where I can use that', 'I'm confident with that part; now on to the next step' and 'Yes, I can implement that tomorrow.'

## PARTICIPANTS SHOW THEY KNOW

Participants benefit from showing their trainer and fellow participants that they are learning. They show they know. They also see others learning, building social proof of the benefit of the new skills and knowledge.

In his book *Influence: Science and Practice* social scientist Robert B. Cialdini discusses six of the commonly occurring patterns of behaviour that most of us fall into in our daily lives. One such pattern Cialdini defines as 'social proof'. Social proof says to us that others around us like something, do something, want something or need something; this influences us to like, do, want or need the same thing. It is the same with training. Often it is only on breaks that participants share how they are feeling about the course, its content and the trainer. Trainers always hope that these are positive feelings.

Review activities help bring positive social proof back into the training room, often as a by-product of the actual process of review. Consider the 'hot tips' review activity, where participants write down their top ten learnings from the course to that point. With this excellent review strategy participants go back through their notes, workbooks and any other material to find their own personal hot tips. When a participant listens to another participant's hot tips and says 'Oh yes, that was good, I'll add that one to my list', it is social proof in action! If most of the group put down a particular topic area as one they thought was terrific, this may influence others to think in a similar way. This is not manipulation of participants but simply recognition of a naturally occurring social pattern of behaviour that we all display.

### AM I THE ONLY ONE WHO'S EXHAUSTED?

I recently attended a training course conducted by a highly acclaimed author and presenter. The group of participants was made up of professional trainers. The day was filled with great content and I was engrossed. However, by mid-afternoon I was exhausted. It took all my effort to write notes and, by the end of the day, the content was a blur.

I was not the only participant to feel like this. As trainers, we were ruthlessly critical of the presenter's style and concluded that this could have been prevented to some extent if the most basic of reviews had been part of the program. The presenter could simply have asked everyone every hour to spend five minutes telling the person next to us what we had learnt. This technique of putting the 'brain in reverse', letting people refuel and having them reflect on their notes, summarise them in a couple of key points and articulate them would have made a tremendous difference.

The point is that regardless of how many people there are in a training session, the duration of the course or the content, the most basic review (like this one, needing no preparation) can be of huge benefit. All you, as a trainer, need is the courage to stop talking!

## PARTICIPANTS 'TEST-DRIVE' IN A SAFE ENVIRONMENT

If the training environment has been set up in a way that encourages participants to participate freely in activities without fear of reprimand if they make mistakes, their willingness to try out new concepts and ideas in a practical way will grow. This point is extremely important. Regardless of how many review activities you put into a training course, if the environment is one based on fear, testing, reprimand or 'reporting back', the quality of the outcome of the review activity will be lower than you expect.

### HOW TO CREATE A SAFE TRAINING ENVIRONMENT

As a trainer you have the power to create your own safe training environment. Many trainers I work with feel they must use the training room in exactly the way it was set up, but this is not so. Make the training room your own, and you will feel more at home.

Before the beginning of each course I train, I spend at least 15 minutes moving desks, chairs and flip-chart stands, cleaning up and putting away things that I am not going to use. Having only what I need reduces distractions. So if I'm not using overhead transparencies

I move the overhead projector either outside the room or to the back of the room. This setting-up procedure helps both the participants and me to focus. Your participants will also appreciate a training room that has been set up specifically to meet their needs.

Strategies for creating a safe environment should start at the beginning of the course during the welcome phase. Tell participants that there are no tests, that they are free to experiment, that the training room is a great place to make mistakes and that we can all learn from our mistakes.

## TAKING THE TEST-DRIVE PHILOSOPHY 'TO THE MAX'

In order to create an environment that is patently free of the 'test' mentality, I go as far as telling my participants that during my courses they can cheat as much as they like. I then pause, usually eliciting sighs of relief and wry smiles all around. I go on to say: 'You can cheat as much as you like to get the answers you need. You can crib from me, from each other, from your workbooks, from the flip charts that I'll be using — any way you like so that you get through the course. If you see someone doing something that you like the look of, or can use, copy that idea and use it for yourself.' Throughout the day, I hear things like 'I'm stuck, can I crib from you?' and when an opposing team catches them looking through their notes during a competitive review activity, they say 'Catherine said we could cheat!' Some trainers don't like the word 'cheat' and that's okay; it works for me and for many other trainers too. I use it because it is so contrary to what we learnt in school, and many adults respond well to this. Sometimes, however, I set an activity where participants need to work alone and without any materials. For such activities I tell participants that 'this is a time when you can't cheat'. They are always okay with this and never do!

The point is to set up an adult learning environment, much like the actual work environment. Many choose to do their activities without cheating, resorting only to reference manuals and the like as a last resort. It never ceases to amaze me how tough adults are on themselves to perform without cheating. My participants know that they are encouraged and rewarded for correctness and accuracy, whether or not they had to look in a reference manual. For me, their results are not measured on memory but on their ability to do the task.

## OTHER WAYS OF CREATING A SAFE LEARNING ENVIRONMENT

Other ways of creating a safe environment include simply having a closed room, where people outside can't see in through windows to office areas. Often, as an external trainer, I have been shown to my training room to find that it has clear glass doors or windows. I carry large sheets of black paper in my flip-chart carry case, which I use to cover the glass up to eye level so that people in my room know that others outside can't see them. This also reduces distractions from passers-by. Of course, nothing I have my participants do is so revealing that they should be locked away! However, during discussions, activities and when they are working on high-concentration areas, the last thing they (or I as their trainer) need is to have their concentration broken. By the first break I have usually posted flip charts that I have used in the previous session over the black paper to lessen the obviousness of the covering.

It's these little things that you do that all add up to creating an environment where learning can really take flight. I encourage you to invest 15 minutes at the beginning of each training course to focus on your training room and create a safe environment for your participants. I also encourage you to explain to your participants that the course is free of tests and exams. Try telling them they can cheat — it does work! This approach will pay off during your training course — for them and for you.

## BENEFIT TO THE TRAINER

Imagine being a fly on the wall of your training room. Imagine being able to fly down and listen to the comments of participants and tap into their emotional state during the course. Imagine being able to buzz around and look at the training environment from all angles. Just imagine the information you'd collect. During a review activity, when participants are completing their task, the trainer is just that — a fly on the wall.

### THE TRAINER AS A 'FLY ON THE WALL'
Throughout the review activity, trainers benefit from observing, listening and working with participants. For this time, trainers are outsiders.

Trainers observe what topic areas in the review activity participants are confident with. During this time, trainers have a golden opportunity to hone their listening and observation skills — noticing things like who in the group is doing the work, who is taking the lead, who is lagging behind, who is drifting along with the group, who is driving the activity. Trainers are also looking for the parts of the review that participants can do easily and with confidence. Often participants will skip hard questions, leaving them until the end. Trainers, in their 'fly on the wall' role, take note, without commenting or interrupting the process, of which ones they are leaving until the end. This is soft data for trainers to collect during the course.

### SEARCHING FOR GAPS IN LEARNING
Trainers are also searching for gaps in participants' learning. Much of the role of a trainer during a review activity is to detect where participants are not confident with the content taught. This benefits the trainer because the gaps in learning are quickly revealed, something that would rarely happen without a review activity. These gaps can then be targeted by the trainer and filled at the time, during the debrief or later in the course.

### CREATING AN ENERGISED GROUP OF PARTICIPANTS
What is most important, with participants who are more confident and energised, trainers

save training time. Don't forget the back-to-basics idea of having a short break every hour. Adult learning theory teaches trainers that participants should break every 50 minutes and that learning declines after this time. The traditional morning and afternoon tea breaks with a rushed lunch depletes participants of energy and lowers the level of learning from after lunch to the end of the day. Most trainers who are committed to learner-centred training structure their courses around sessions of between 50 and 60 minutes. Mini-breaks of 5 to 10 minutes are scheduled throughout the day with a one-hour break for lunch. This gives participants time to have a solid break and attend to necessary phone calls etc. This break strategy helps to conserve energy and keep learning levels high.

## SAVING TIME BY PUTTING IN REVIEW ACTIVITIES

As learners, we know that if it is not relevant to our lives learning takes us longer and is more of a struggle. We also know that if we are feeling confident, adding another piece of information to our knowledge base is easier than when we are feeling low, uninspired or lacking in confidence.

Review activities keep the relevance and confidence levels high throughout the entire course. By reviewing content learnt at least every hour, participants' confidence levels are kept high. By continuously looking for ways to apply the learning, participants are keeping the learning relevant. These two things, relevance and confidence, contribute to a faster learning pace for participants. So if your participants are learning faster with review activities than without them, you, the trainer, are saving time. In Chapter 7, I explain how to schedule review activities throughout the training day.

As far as time goes, review activities are self-accommodating. Because reviews contribute to a faster pace of learning, the time taken to run the review does not add to the training day but rather is absorbed into the day. Here is a working example of adding reviews without losing content or time:

If you have traditionally run courses with one morning and one afternoon tea-break, your training sessions will be up to two hours long (say between 10.30 a.m. and 12.30 p.m.). There are no review activities, only mini-lectures and some hands-on activities where the learner fills in a workbook or tries the new content for the first time.

One way to increase learning immediately is to convert that two-hour session into two shorter sessions (10.30–11.20 a.m., break for ten minutes, then 11.30 a.m.–12.30 p.m.). The break, during which participants have refreshments and do some physical movement, will re-energise them. As a result, when they re-enter the training room learning levels will increase because of the increased energy. The ten minutes will make up for itself because the rate of learning in the second hour is increased.

The task of putting in review activities works the same way as the breaks. Let's say you now have two sessions, namely 10.30–11.20 a.m. and 11.30 a.m.–12.30 p.m. You may choose to add a five-minute review activity related to the topic taught in that session between 11.15 and 11.20 a.m. Participants go to the break knowing that they know the material that has been taught in that 45 minutes.

Because of the successful outcome of the review, confidence levels are up. Some participants may spend time during the break thinking some more about that topic or discussing it with others, and that's even better.

After the break (at 11.30 a.m.) you may choose to add another five-minute review activity; this time one of reflection. By spending five minutes on 'how will you apply what you have learnt', participants again review the 45-minute topic and tell others how they will apply their learning. This invokes social proof and commitment to the topic and improves the learning pace for the next topic, which starts at 11.35 a.m. It also gives participants an opportunity to clarify any final questions, some of which may have arisen at the break.

At 12.20 p.m. you may choose to do a pre-lunch review activity reviewing aspects from all topics trained so far. This ten-minute review may take the form of a whole group true/false activity. This is usually a quick activity and is ideal for consolidating participants' knowledge in a energetic way prior to lunch.

## SUMMARY OF HOW REVIEW ACTIVITIES SAVE TIME

Review activities build social proof, confidence and relevance, which influences adults to learn at a faster rate than if the opposite emotional state were in place. If you use frequent breaks, you will find that because of the higher rate of learning you are delivering the same amount of content in a much shorter time. This saving in time is reinvested in the time taken to conduct review activities. It is an amazing paradox that time-strapped trainers can add review activities to an existing session without adding to the time taken to run them.

# BENEFIT TO THE ORGANISATION

Organisations pay either directly or indirectly for training courses, so they expect the goals of a training course to be met and to see a corresponding change in behaviour from those who attend the course. Organisations expect change to occur after a training course — if they didn't they wouldn't pay for them! This is quite an obvious point, on the surface, but there are many hidden complexities. Questions like: 'How does the organisation know whether the goals of the training course have been met?' and 'How does the organisation track the behaviour change in employees attending training?' have often left the professional trainer in a quandary. Most trainers either expect or assume that some sort of post-course evaluation will be conducted back in the workplace by the participants' manager. The trainer, doing their own post-course evaluation, may support this process.

Review activities and their results can greatly enhance the quality of information that is available to an organisation as feedback. The outcome of a review activity provides data on the standard of the participants' knowledge. This data can be collected quickly and efficiently. A simple table can be created listing each participant's name, and each of the review activities being conducted in the training course. Each review activity has its own column and space for comments. If a participant meets all the success criteria for an activity a tick can be placed in that column. If a gap is found, the trainer notes it during the next break. This provides a great record for the trainer, the training department and the organisation as a whole.

Imagine the benefit to a large organisation if this vast amount of data were available and used in a proactive way. It could then be fed into the company's performance management system, manager coaching and other focus areas for employee development, not to mention raising the profile, visibility and credibility of the training department.

Organisations expect that learning from a training course will be transferred to the workplace. Some organisations participate in making this happen. During a review activity, the learning is still under the supervision and guidance of the trainer, who is witnessing the beginning of the transfer of learning. This gives the trainer an indication of how the participant will apply their learning in the workplace.

## SUMMARY

The professional trainer is a little like an orchestra conductor. The trainer guides the participant through the learning process and through the first stages of application, knowing that the participant is confident to go it alone after the training is finished. At the end of the training, it is quite common for a participant and the organisation to forget the process of training altogether and to focus on the improvement. And that's okay! It is a lot like remembering the wonderful music played with little concern for the effort of the conductor! Each individual participant will have their own individual and unique experience of your training course that comes together in the workplace in the form of improvement for the organisation. Creating opportunity for others to succeed needs to be the primary aim of the professional adult educator — whether or not the audience openly cheers your efforts!

# CHAPTER THREE

## MYTHS ABOUT MEASURING LEARNING

* CAN LEARNING BE MEASURED DURING THE TRAINING?

* DOES A WRITTEN EXAM MEASURE LEARNING?

* NO TIME FOR REVIEWS?

Myths surround the measuring of learning for many reasons — fear of the unknown, fear of accountability, fear of up-to-date training styles and fear of expanding our own knowledge in adult education. For some reason, in many organisations it seems acceptable for a trainer to walk into a training room, train and walk out, tell their manager 'Yes, the course was good' and not to have to measure how the investment in that training has contributed to the organisation. As business becomes more accountable in all areas of operation, so too must the professional trainer take responsibility for ensuring that what is learnt in the training room is applied in the workplace.

## EXPLORING THE COMMON MYTHS

There are four common myths surrounding measuring learning:
1. Learning can't be measured during a training course; it can only be successfully measured back at the workplace.
2. A written test or exam at the end of the course measures the adult learner's knowledge.
3. An evaluation form at the end of the course is a measure of learning.
4. There is so much content to get through, there's no time left for reviews.

Each of these myths warrants further exploration. In this chapter keep in mind that the key words are 'measuring' and 'learning'.

## MYTH 1: LEARNING CAN'T BE MEASURED DURING A TRAINING COURSE

How do we know whether participants are capable of applying new skills and ideas in their jobs? Learning measures must be taken during the training course if you want to be able to say you know they know.

### THINGS OVERHEARD FROM TRAINERS
Too often, trainers simply guess at participants' abilities. After a course, trainers have said things like: 'Sally will go okay', 'Juan is going really well; I wish there were more like him', 'Bill has no idea', 'Betty will probably leave. This change is too much for her.' These trainers generally have no future contact with their participants and are generally those who do not measure training during the training course. It's usually unconscious incompetence on their parts — they don't know what they don't know. The following questions will help you to discover what you do not know, and may even expose a level of conscious incompetence. They may also reinforce your conscious competence. Either way, I trust that you will strive ultimately to become unconsciously competent!

## QUESTIONS TO ASK YOURSELF TO OVERCOME MYTH 1

### 1. What's the difference between 'care' and 'genuine care'?

Trainers do care about their participants, their course and their role as trainers. Trainers who genuinely care assume the responsibility of ensuring that participants are ready. During review activities participants are proving to themselves and the trainer that they have learnt, retained and are ready to apply their learning. The trainer charged with this responsibility wants to measure the training during the course and does not leave it until participants return to the workplace to find out the result. Ask yourself:

- Do you genuinely care if your participants learn, retain and are ready to apply their learning?
- If so, what specific things are you actively doing in your training courses to show this?
- What tangible evidence do you have to prove to yourself and others that your participants can and are ready to apply their learning?

### 2. How much time do I take to measure learning?

Most professional trainers no longer lecture endlessly. They create activities for participants to do to try out new skills, and exercises that actively bring the learning about. Most trainers look for the results of these activities, but perhaps they only give participants time to test-drive their new skills once. Guided exercises and activities allow the trainer to know that the participant can produce a result in a guided way — not in an unguided way, which is what will be expected at the end of the course. This one-time learning is activity-based learning and it is indeed a step better than endless lecturing!

But what if the trainer scheduled several 'pitstops' during the course to check and truly measure participants' progress? If a trainer genuinely cares and assumes responsibility they will include time to get a true indication of whether the participant is ready to apply the learning. The trainer will create semi-guided and unguided activities where the participant can fully explore the learning and relate it to their work. The professional trainer will record the information relating to the work so that it can be used by other areas of the organisation: by human resources staff, line managers, coaches, as part of a mentoring system or to assist in organisational development. Ask yourself:

- Do you check and measure the progress of each individual participant throughout the course?
- If so, what is the balance of time between learning new content and checking that your participants truly know that content?
- Do you have an administration system in place to capture this data?
- If so, how is that information used to support the ongoing development of your participants when they return to their workplace?

### 3. How can I create a state of knowing they know?

I tell my participants that I don't have extrasensory perception. If they need to know something, they must let me know! Of course, I use many strategies to determine what participants need; however, my reminding them that I don't have ESP indicates that my training is a two-way relationship — they need to help me to help them.

A trainer who genuinely cares and has included training measures during the course is a step closer to knowing exactly what level of confidence, knowledge and understanding participants have, and can therefore make better and more targeted judgments and decisions about the path that their course will take. A trainer with this knowledge can change course like a well-informed navigator. A trainer without this knowledge could be sailing in circles or into a storm without knowing. By changing the training course, a trainer can help to ensure that participants will apply the learning into the workplace. Ask yourself:

- Do you know the exact level each of your participants is at throughout the training course?
- If so, how do you know?
- How much is hearsay and guessing and how much is based on solid evidence?

## 4. How do I create a strategy for participants who don't measure up?

For many participants in traditional training courses, it is possible to sit through the course, participate in just enough activities to get through and leave without learning much at all. The traditional trainer, whose goal it is to 'get through the course' will allow this to happen. Where these participants were not ready or not skilled enough to apply what they learnt, the problem does not go away. In cases like this, when the participant returns to the workplace they demonstrate no change in behaviour and may attract negative attention. There may be other consequences for the training department, the person who authorised the participant to go on the course and, perhaps, the trainer. Sadly, often the trainer gets off scot-free.

Trainers who genuinely care have included training measures during the course, and can change the course based on reliable information about participants' confidence levels and ability to apply their learning. They are on track to knowing they know. The trainer who takes responsibility for filling gaps in the participant's learning during the course will really make a difference to each and every participant they train. Ask yourself:

- Do you have a strategy for participants who need further help?
- If so, can you clearly articulate your strategy?
- If you do not have a formal strategy for participants who need help, what do you do when participants require assistance?

## 5. Who can help me?

In many organisations performance management systems are successfully in place. Other initiatives include coaching by managers, mentoring programs and other employee development opportunities. In many organisations the training and development function plays an important role in linking with the findings of these programs and often plays an integral part in the ongoing development of employees. Many organisations, however, do not link these functions. The growing trend of trainers working directly with employees and their managers raises the profile of the training function and can be seen as adding value back into the organisation.

An organisation that I have worked closely with for some years is reworking their performance management system so that when a development opportunity arises for an employee, their internal training department has a training course to fill that gap. On the surface, that's not difficult; however, consider all of the employee positions in a large organisation and all of the potential development opportunities that may occur! This is a major initiative that will span several years in its development, and the outcome should prove most rewarding. It will create a training and development function within the organisation that will be an integral part of the development of all employees, managers and senior executives. It will mean that during a training course, the trainer will have a range of options when a participant requires further assistance. The trainer can enlist the help of the participant's manager to provide ongoing coaching to ensure their learning is applied in the workplace.

When a trainer genuinely cares, has included training measures during the course, makes changes to the course based on reliable information and assumes the responsibility to fill the gaps, the participant is likely to be ready to apply their learnings in the workplace. However, when a trainer is working with the participant's manager to ensure the learnings are applied, a positive result is virtually guaranteed. It is a joint effort by all the parties involved. Generally, to introduce such systems in large organisations is a huge task requiring formal commitment from all levels of management. As a consultant to organisations, I do not always have the influence to create this standard. However, regardless of the size of organisation you work for or if you consult to organisations, steps can be taken to create a similar outcome.

The first step is to find out who the participant's manager is. When a client sends me a list of participant names, I ask that they include the manager's name as well. When the pre-course pack is sent to participants (questionnaire, course outline, logistics of the course and information sheet), we also send a pack for each manager. This includes a letter detailing the goals of the course, a course outline and information about their role. We ask the manager to meet with the participant to discuss their personal goals and objectives for the course and we give the manager a list of questions to help them with this process.

When the participant arrives at the course, they are clear on their focus areas. This process is as much for the participant and the manager as it is for the trainer. Having a participant who is focused on what they need to learn and why they need to learn it, saves me training time because participants' focus is sharpened.

This process is not difficult or time consuming and should not be avoided. The benefit is twofold. First, the participant and the manager are well informed and well prepared for the course. Second, after the course, I can talk directly to the manager knowing that they are involved in and committed to the the learning process. As a result, the manager is more likely to be receptive to assisting the participant (and the trainer) with ongoing coaching to help fill remaining gaps in learning. Ask yourself:

- Do you engage participants' managers in an active way in ongoing coaching sessions?
- If so, what is the communication strategy between the manager and you, the participant's trainer?
- If not, how does the manager know what the participant is expected to be mastering and when to step in and help?

With these, and the other questions in this section, take some time to reflect on your answers, and if your answers are mixed, then don't worry, you're not alone!

### A FINAL NOTE ON MYTH 1

When I pose these and other difficult questions to professional educators, generally the answers are not quickly formed. Recently, a team of trainers I work with decided that these questions were worthy of serious attention and scheduled a strategic planning day on which they focused on these areas. The answers seemed quite easy on the surface; however, much time, energy and commitment were required over a long period of time to implement the answers in their corporate training environment. The benefit to them is that now they can answer these questions in a positive way and with absolute clarity. The knock-on benefit has been a sharp increase in retention and application of content by their training participants. Their investment of time and effort has had an outstanding return.

If you dedicate yourself to ensuring that strategies and work practices are in place during the training course, the odds of successful learning transfer to the workplace are greater. Furthermore, post-course evaluation and measurement becomes richer and more valuable. Relationships between the trainer, the participant and their manager, together with other internal and external customers, will be greatly enhanced as you all strive to get the maximum outcome from the course content and apply it back in the workplace.

## MYTH 2: A WRITTEN TEST OR EXAM MEASURES LEARNING

In the past few years, trainers, theorists, university students and researchers have written many books and papers about adults and how they learn. These books and papers have covered subject domains such as adult emotions and emotional responses to learning and learning environments. When I was at school, I rarely studied. I had little interest in science and mathematics, preferring to spend my time on art, music or debating. Like many others, I studied the night before exams, regurgitating the material the next day. Did I actually learn science, mathematics, biology or history? No!

**A HORROR STORY**

As a professional trainer, I find the following true story quite shocking, so, as they say in Hollywood, I have changed some details to protect the innocent! Recently, I was involved in the redesign of a series of highly technical computer courses. These courses formed part of a massive technological, organisational, cultural and workplace change. Most of the training courses went for five days continuously. Participants would arrive on Monday, knowing nothing of the new system and by Friday be expected to be experts. The training rooms were set up with 15 computers per room, but participants often had to share computers. In each room was one trainer and sometimes a second trainer was scheduled to help with practical exercises. Both trainers had themselves only just learnt the new system. The training rooms had no spare space whatsoever, no windows and, because of their location, the only option for lunch was dial-in pizzas. You get the picture!

One particular trainer in this huge rollout of technology was conducting a two-hour closed-book exam on the new computer system at the end of the five-day training course. The participants were told first thing Monday morning that they would be having an exam on the Friday. The scene was set for nervous regurgitation of material 'learnt'. It is worthwhile exploring the following difficult questions:

1. **Did this exam measure what participants remembered on the training day?**
   Yes. On the Friday participants answered the questions to the best of their ability. They could not use any reference material or their computers and relied on their memory. So, in essence, the exam did measure what the participants could remember that day.

2. **Did this exam measure what participants learnt?**
   No. The course went for five days and there was considerable opportunity for participants to learn throughout that time. They had ample resource material, including workbooks, on-line help and the help of their trainer. This exam removed all of those resources and created a tense atmosphere. It could be argued that the exam was testing learning, but because of the pressure-cooker environment that was created it was unfair to expect measures to truly reflect the amount these adults had learnt.

3. **Did this exam measure how well participants will apply the material back at their workplace?**
   No. There was no correlation between the exam and how the material would be applied in the workplace. When I asked the trainer who wrote the exam to list the main things participants needed to survive on the job, he didn't know. The trainer had been told to train the participants in everything in that part of the system. So the exam contained questions accordingly, without prioritisation relative to on-the-job application. The questions were also system-based questions (like, what is the third item of a particular menu?) not questions on how the participant would use the system.

4. **Was there a genuine interest in how participants would be able to adapt to their changing work environment with a new computer system, changed job roles and new teams of people to interact with?**

No. The trainer had never worked in the areas in which his participants worked, nor had he ever fully explored their job functions. There was little or no communication strategy worked out about the change to the work environment, how the job roles would change and how the new systems would be implemented. The training focused on the technical keystroke-by-keystroke ability of the participants.

5. **Could the trainer get 100% if they sat the exam?**

When I asked the trainer this question, he admitted that even he wouldn't be able to get 100% in the exam. He had been working with the system for longer than the participants, had undergone training provided by the software company that wrote the program, had written the training course and written the exam. Under Myth 1 I discussed genuine care and responsibility on the part of the trainer and, clearly, this approach was not much in evidence in this situation.

6. **Did the results of the exam affect the participants' job prospects and were they relayed to senior managers in the organisation?**

Yes. The senior team of managers whose objective it was to ensure the project succeeded was very interested in the results of the exam. One participant, prior to the results being published, made an appointment with the human resources manager to discuss her fear of a poor result and to discuss what the repercussions of such a result might be. The participant, who was a top performer on the job, had explained during the meeting that she had always had shocking exam nerves and had been like that all through school too. The participant was concerned that her results would be reflected in her HR file. The HR manager assured the participant that she had nothing to fear and reported back to the trainer that this meeting had taken place.

The participant did not do well in the exam, the results were relayed to the senior team and other managers in her group. Some weeks later the participant was fired for non-performance. The exam results were considered by her manager to be concrete evidence that she was unable to cope with the new system.

7. **Was the exam result a true indication of how well the participant would use the computer system on the job?**

Definitely not! On the job, participants could access on-line help, their reference manuals, training aids, other people in their team, ring the help desk and numerous other ways of getting the task done. The exam was a tick-in-the-box method, so the trainers could report back to the senior team that the participants knew the technical work. The exam was trainer-centred, not learner-centred. Who knows how much the participants learnt and what really happened to them both during the exam and back on the job.

### SUMMARY OF EXAM-STYLE ENVIRONMENT

Professional trainers know that some adults do well at exams and tests and others do not. The results an adult gets may or may not be truly aligned to the amount of learning that has taken place. Rarely does the exam environment mirror the environment in which the learning will be applied.

On the job, the participant has all sorts of formal ways to find answers to their problems — reference material, help desks, training aids and so on. Significantly, many adults are skilled at building informal networks of people from whom they can seek help. Exams and tests only measure what is remembered on the day, not necessarily what has been learnt.

Avoiding the exam-style environment should be a top-of-the-list priority for all professional trainers. Learning can be successfully measured without this pressure, using review activities and post-course learning measures. The results of these measures will not only be better, they will be more accurate. I am confident that given the chance all trainers would rather relay better and more accurate results that can be backed up by solid data to a participant's manager than the often inaccurate results of a closed-book examination.

## WHAT ABOUT INDUSTRY-SET EXAMS AND COMPLIANCE REGULATIONS?

If training must close with a formal assessment trainers should take a proactive approach to ensuring their participants are confindent, skilled and ready to sit the exam. If they undergo regular review activities throughout the course and sit preparatory exams, most participants will tend to accept even the most rigorous exam.

# MYTH 3: AN EVALUATION FORM IS A MEASURE OF LEARNING

Have you ever thought about why evaluation forms are often called smile sheets? One trainer I know announces, 'Here's your smile sheet to fill in. Make sure you're nice!' As a trainer, how often do you ever see a poor evaluation form? Most trainers know that if they get a bad evaluation form, something has really gone wrong for that participant. Mostly, there is one of two reactions: ignore the bad evaluation (it was their problem!) or spiral into a decline and reconsider your career choice as a trainer (a bit dramatic, but you get the point!).

When we were children, our parents taught us some fundamental lessons about how to behave and how to treat the teachers at school. The teachers themselves reinforced these lessons, and so shaped the way I conducted myself as a student. These lessons were 'hard-wired' in my brain as a child and now, as an adult, I act in a similar way when I am in a learning environment. I may be older, more skilled, no longer a 'student' but a 'participant', but for me and many other adults, the lessons are still in force. The myth of evaluation forms being a measure of learning can be illustrated by looking at just some of these lessons my parents and indeed most parents taught their children.

### 'Be nice to your teacher'

Participants are generally gracious people who have been taught not to hurt other people's feelings. They know that the trainer will read the evaluation form. They believe that, regardless of their skill and competence, the trainer probably tried their best. If the trainer is internal and working in the same organisation as them, the participant knows that they will be likely to meet the trainer again, or even work with them in a future position within the organisation. If the trainer is external, the participant knows the company paid a fee for them to do the training and that whoever booked the training will be accountable for how that money was spent. All these things influence participants to be gracious on the evaluation form.

### 'Teachers know more than you'

When I was in high school, mathematics was not my best subject, and I thought that there was something wrong with me. I didn't get it! Yet, as an adult, my maths is just fine. Like schoolchildren, adult participants often think 'It's my fault I didn't get that part of the course. I couldn't have been concentrating — I have always been hopeless at this stuff', and other self-deprecating thoughts. So when it comes to completing an evaluation form, often these thoughts persist in the minds of the participants. Participants will often globalise their responses to include such things as 'the course was delivered well' with perhaps an invisible 'but I didn't get it'. If evaluation forms do focus on learning-type questions, participants will rarely want to reveal that 'they didn't get it' because of the unknown consequences that such a comment might have. It's easy to see that evaluation forms do not always reflect the true responses of participants.

### 'If you can't say anything nice, don't say anything at all'

Rarely do participants ever write anything other than good things about the trainer and the content of the course. They will leave a section blank when they have nothing flattering to write. As a training manager, when I look at other trainers' evaluation forms and my own, I know that the less there is written the more worried I should be. It is because of this ingrained lesson that evaluation forms are often accurately called 'smile sheets'.

## WHAT ARE EVALUATION FORMS EXPECTED TO MEASURE?

In organisations across the world, evaluation forms are used to measure the trainer's competence, the content of the course and how much learning has taken place. However, depending on its content, the evaluation form may not measure these three things at all. Evaluation forms generally evaluate the execution of the training course, its administration, the trainer and the content presented, but they do not and cannot measure learning.

However, it is the expectation of many organisations that evaluations do, in fact, measure learning. For many, the results of evaluation forms influence the number of courses run, development programs for trainers, whether a training department should be internal or external and even how successful a training department is. These and many other important decisions about the future of trainers, training departments and participants are often made using evaluation forms as the only source of data.

## EVALUATION FORMS MEASURING TRAINER COMPETENCE

In many instances evaluation forms do not accurately reflect the competence of the trainer. As discussed, participants generally either write positive things about a trainer or leave that section blank. So to measure the competence of a trainer based on these measures is a somewhat misguided enterprise. Organisations should devise other methods to accurately measure the effectiveness and competence of a trainer. These methods could provide valuable data to a training manager and their organisation. The knock-on effect is a higher standard of training for all employees.

## EVALUATION FORMS MEASURING CONTENT

Evaluation forms do not measure the suitability of the content or its contribution to the participant and the organisation. Evaluation forms often have tick-in-the-box measures for how relevant a course is to the participant. For this section and many others an individual's perceptions are relied on. My definition of highly relevant, somewhat relevant and so on could be completely different from that of the participant sitting next to me. Also, with new learning it may not be until a participant returns to the workplace that they fully understand the relevance of the course for them. Take for instance a new manager who goes on a course and is expected to start a new position once she completes it. Certainly, the person has some idea of how they will apply their learning, but they can't fully know its relevance until they are back at their workplace and in their new position. This is why these types of questions are probably more suited to post-course evaluation than in-course evaluation.

Things never learnt can never be applied. If a participant simply attends the teaching of a topic but does not get a chance to practise their skills the trainer can't know if they know. Proof of learning in a controlled environment, such as a training room, is an important indicator of the success the participant might have in the workplace.

## IF EVALUATION FORMS DON'T MEASURE LEARNING, WHAT DOES?

Only review activities run at regular intervals throughout the training course and post-course measures have a chance at measuring what participants have learnt. Review activities can measure what participants know at the time of learning. When a trainer conducts a review activity both the participant and the trainer have the opportunity to reflect on the result and, if there are gaps in their learning, work together to fill those gaps.

Reviews also measure the readiness of the participant to apply their learning. A review in the reflective style of 'how will you use this information' can assist the trainer to collect soft data on how the participant expects to apply their learning when they return to their job. This data can assist the trainer to confidently discuss with others, say the participant's manager, how the participant expects to increase their competence in the workplace.

The outcome of review activities can provide valuable data against which participants and trainers can be measured. The data that they provide needs to be combined with other information to compile a complete picture of competence.

### SO, DO I THROW OUT THE EVALUATION FORMS?

Evaluation forms are evidence of attendance and a first-line general opinion of how the course went for participants. As your first step, you could simply combine the results of review activities with those of evaluation forms. This is a step in the right direction for creating valuable information for participants, trainers and the organisation. Some time in the future, you may decide on a completely different evaluation process, which doesn't use your traditional evaluation form at all or uses an enhanced version of it. In the mean time, however, I would suggest taking small steps and testing systems bit by bit, to ultimately reach a higher standard of course evaluation that does measure learning.

## MYTH 4: THERE'S NO TIME LEFT FOR REVIEWS

The issue of time was discussed in Chapter 2. I included a working example of how reviews can be added to the course without sacrificing content and saving time as a result. Even with this knowledge, the time-strapped trainer will be tempted to drop a review from the course in order to get through the content and finish on time. The question must be asked: For whose sake are you dropping the review? There are only three answers, that of the participant, the organisation or the trainer.

As far as time goes, review activities are self-accommodating. Owing to the faster pace of learning, the time taken to run the review does not add to the training day but is rather absorbed into the day. The learning pace quickens because of the social proof that is operating in the training room, the high level of confidence on the part of participants and the usefulness or relevance of the material being learnt.

As a professional trainer, my goal is that by the end of my training courses my participants know 100%, or close to it, of all the topics covered. The only way I know this is to see evidence of it for myself, and the outcome of review activities helps me to know they know. However, there comes a time when a choice has to be made: content versus knowing they know. I have a certain amount of training content to cover during the course and my course objectives reflect this expectation. What's important for a trainer whose focus is the learner is to ensure that the learner is confident and able to apply the material taught.

## WHAT IF YOU GET BEHIND SCHEDULE?

When I am behind schedule, I would rather ensure that my participants are confident and able to apply say, 19 out of the 20 topics, than risk putting in the twentieth topic, which may leave them confused without any time for me to remedy that confusion. Such confusion could adversely affect their state of mind when they leave the training course, which could, in turn, have negative repercussions when it comes to applying the 19 topics that they were once confident with. The twentieth topic isn't as important to me as knowing that my participants are fully confident and able to apply the 19 that went before it.

### WAYS OF TEACHING THE MISSING CONTENT

So what happens to the twentieth topic? Usually, whatever topic number it is, it probably takes between 15 minutes and 45 minutes to train. There are many options available to trainers. At least some of these will be available to you. These options include scheduling another short session to cover this topic and sending self-directed learning packs to participants so they can do it in their own time. In this case, the post-course review will need to check that they have done this self-directed work. Other more technical options include sending a video or audiocassette of the training to each participant, using web-based training by posting the training session on the Internet or an intranet or holding a video conference. You could also train the twentieth topic as part of another course that you know participants will be attending or simply not train it at all. There are several other options and what you do will be determined in part by your resources and overall training schedule.

### MAKING JUDGMENTS ABOUT THE WORTH OF THE CONTENT

I always ask myself — I hope not cynically — if it's the last topic of a training course, is it vital anyway? This is a difficult question, the response to which can't be generalised. Sometimes the last topic is essential, other times it is just good to know. You, the professional trainer, need to make that decision at the time of training; however, I would urge you not to risk a drop in participants' confidence levels by cramming in more content, just so you can say you've done everything in your course outline.

## A FINAL NOTE ON MYTH 4

The bottom line is this — you don't have time not to have time for review activities! If your purpose is to have confident participants who are ready to apply their learning and you are centred on the learner then you will create time. If you are conducting a content-rich course that doesn't have review activities, you can add them to your course without scheduling additional time. If you are ever behind time, I strongly recommend that you drop content before dropping a review activity. It's better for your participants to be confident and ready to apply everything you have taught them than confused and overwhelmed a mass of content and no opportunity to check understanding.

## SUMMARY

These myths about learning are firmly entrenched in some people's minds, but remember what I've said in this chapter. Embrace change if you need to. Both you and your participants will reap the rewards.

# CHAPTER FOUR

# LINKING REVIEW ACTIVITIES TO COURSE GOALS

* STEP 1: WRITING YOUR COURSE GOALS

* STEP 2: SETTING SUCCESS CRITERIA FOR REVIEW ACTIVITIES

* STEP 3: SETTING MULTI-LEVEL OBJECTIVES FROM HANDS-ON REVIEW ACTIVITIES

Linking your review activities to the overall goals of the course is of the utmost importance. But before we look at how to link them, let's consider what content style your review activities may take.

# CHOOSING THE CONTENT STYLE OF THE REVIEW ACTIVITY

The first consideration in choosing an appropriate review activity is to think about the type of training course and the style of content that you are about to train. The styles of content will often drive the choice of review activity; however, with some adaptation, most of the review activities that I have included later in this book will work with your content.

## HUMAN RESOURCE DEVELOPMENT CONTENT

For the purposes of this book I have used the term 'human resource development' or HRD to broadly describe courses that are non-technical in nature, for example change management, selling, customer service, leadership, train-the-trainer, presentation skills and other theoretical, conceptual, attitudinal or behavioural change courses. Often referred to as 'soft skills' or 'people development', these courses are non-technical in nature. In this context, the term in no way relates to the function or department within an organisation that manages training and the development of employees.

### THE ISSUE OF INACTIVITY

One of the key considerations when choosing a review activity is that participants on HRD courses are often sitting at desks for most of the training day. With such inactivity, participants' learning pace will slow and they may become sluggish during the afternoon sessions. So the review activity should not only serve the content objectives, but also provide some physical activity for the participants. This approach re-ignites participants and boosts their energy levels, providing fuel for the remaining training topics.

Even the most basic review activity, such as regrouping your participants into teams of four or five, having them sort review cards and then posting these on the training room wall, helps by having participants move and stretch their bodies.

## TECHNICAL CONTENT

When choosing review activities, give special consideration to technical content such as computer training, hands-on mechanical training, factory training (on plant or equipment), product training or any type of physical step-by-step task.

Review activities are of paramount importance in technical courses and should be conducted at least every hour. Unlike those on HRD courses, participants in technical training are either able or unable to perform a task. There are rarely 'shades of grey' in their skill levels — the only variable is how well they complete the task. Because there is such variation in skill levels, the trainer must be focused on ensuring that participants can confidently do the tasks taught in the training. The trainer must know they know.

## TECHNICAL DATA OVERLOAD

Technical courses are often filled with process-driven information. For two, three and even up to ten days, participants are expected to take in vast amounts of technical data and step-by-step processes. If you consider the amount of learning any one participant is expected to do during a technical training course, compared with the amount of new technical information that same participant learns in the same time span at work, is it any wonder their eyes glaze over?

Adding reviews to a technical training course is a bit like adding phrasing to music. Without phrasing, music would just be a string of notes being played. Phrasing breaks up these notes into passages that help to provide the 'feel' of the music. Just like phrasing in music, review activities provide participants with a break from the expectation that they can absorb endless new material. Review activities act as breathers, where participants can stop and review what they have learnt. This process builds their confidence and readies them for the next step of their journey.

## DIFFERENT FORMS OF TECHNICAL REVIEW ACTIVITIES

Technical review activities can take many forms, but just because your course is technical in nature does not mean you have to stay with computer-based or equipment-based review activity methods. There are many options available to trainers that allow participants to move away from their equipment and engage in small group activities. The fact that you are using equipment such as computers or teaching about a piece of factory equipment is no reason for you and your participants to feel you must be focused on that apparatus for the duration of the training. Participants are always refreshed when they can move away from the computer or other equipment, shifting their focus for a short time before returning.

## HANDS-ON REVIEW ACTIVITY EXERCISES

When included in a technical training course, hands-on review activities that are unguided or semi-guided by the trainer form an excellent basis for the measurement of skills acquired. These review activities should be geared to participants' real working life and can be done alone, in pairs or in teams of up to four participants.

## STEP-BY-STEP PROCESSES

Technical content is often based on a series of step-by-step processes and it is important to realise that these processes can be reviewed either with or without the equipment. The trainer should make this decision based on what would naturally occur in the participants' workplace. By doing so, the trainer ensures that the participants are confident with the steps in the process and are able to measure the outcome.

### BEING RESOURCEFUL IN A STEP-BY-STEP PROCESS

The opportunity to be resourceful (or 'cheat') in these review activities is also important. Rarely would participants be expected to recite the steps of a complex process without the aid of reference material or, say, a computer in the workplace. They also have many other resources on the job — guides, on-line help, other people or simply using the piece of equipment as a prompt. Many of the best computer users can't recite the steps of, say, a mail merge; however, they can confidently do a mail merge when seated at the computer. As a trainer, you can set up this environment by allowing participants to use whatever resource material they have to hand in order to complete the review activity successfully.

### MOVING AWAY FROM THE EQUIPMENT OR COMPUTERS

A key consideration in computer training, for example, is the need for participants to move away from their computers at regular intervals throughout the day. A review activity that involves moving to someone else's computer in a pair-and-share activity or doing a non-computer-based review activity will breathe energy into your training room.

### A TYPICAL COMPUTER TRAINER STORY

Recently, I was conducting a course attended by a large group of computer trainers involved in training word processing, spreadsheets, databases and the like. They had designed their courses without any review activities. When I asked them about writing reviews into their courses they all chorused 'Oh, but this is computer training, there's nothing you can do. Our participants just have to accept that it is boring and it's okay with us if they fall asleep after lunch.' My reaction was outwardly calm, but I'm sure they heard my sigh. Such comments are, unfortunately, not unusual. Even in the most cramped computer training room I can run each of the reviews that I have documented for you with great success. The bottom line is to remember this — there is no review that is conducted in an HRD course that can't be conducted in a computer course. In fact, with the wealth of step-by-step instructions and process-driven tasks these domains entail, creating reviews for technical training is simpler than for HRD training.

## LINKING REVIEW ACTIVITIES TO THE TRAINING COURSE GOALS

Having determined the style of your review activities, next you should consider how to link the review activities to the training course goals.

### WHAT ARE THE GOALS OF THE TRAINING?

Ask yourself: When it is all over, what exactly do you want them to be able to do?

It is important to stress knowing the objective or outcome of the training course as a whole. It's like preparing for a trip — the preparation precedes the actualisation of the goal. In the case of training courses, you need to predetermine the destination that you want your participants to reach by the end of the course. There may be a number of milestones or markers to reach along the way to the ultimate destination and, if so, these should be predetermined as well. Individual success criteria for each review activity can then be written based on the overall course goals. Remember that if you don't know the goal of the course, how will you know when you and your participants have successfully completed the course?

## STEP 1: WRITING YOUR COURSE GOALS

Your first step should be to write down your training goals. This will help later when you are establishing what review activities will be needed. You can also use your training goals to measure accurately whether you successfully achieved what you set out to do. When the training course is over, spend some time reflecting on your overall success.

### WHY BOTHER WITH GOALS?

Some years ago, a training manager asked me: 'What are the course goals?' I talked for a while, trying to give the impression that I was well prepared. The manager then asked whether the goals were written down. I sheepishly remarked that I thought they were, all the while hoping my co-trainer could come to my rescue! The manager then wanted to know whether the goals were up to date and asked for a copy. Luckily, my co-trainer had written them down when he wrote the course and I escaped unscathed. Yet many trainers would be unprepared for this request, thinking that written goals are simply 'nice to haves' for a training course.

What are the goals of the training course? If you don't know what you are trying to achieve, you will not know whether or not you have achieved it. Take time to write down the course goals formally with a view to the practical application of the course material. What is it you want your participants to be able to do once the training course is over?

### HOW COURSE GOALS WILL HELP YOU TO CHOOSE A REVIEW ACTIVITY

The course goals will often drive the choice of a review activity. If it is important to know key terminology, acronyms or step-by-step instructions, your review should focus on these areas. If your course goal is to change behaviours of teams, managers and supervisors, your review activity should focus on team-based reviews where communication skills are of primary importance.

Many trainers find it helpful to write down the course goals using the following worksheet. Some trainers have used this worksheet to create a standard template and have added it to their instructional design kit. The completed worksheet showing the training course goals then forms part of the trainer's guide for use by all trainers of that course.

**FIGURE 4.1** // TRAINING GOALS WORKSHEET

| |
|---|
| **COURSE NAME:** |
| **TRAINER'S NAME:** |
| **DATE:** |
| AT THE END OF THIS COURSE, MY PARTICIPANTS WILL HAVE... |
| AT THE END OF THIS COURSE, I (THE TRAINER) WILL KNOW... |
| THE SHORT-TERM BENEFIT OF COMPLETING THIS COURSE IS... |
| THE LONG-TERM BENEFIT OF COMPLETING THIS COURSE IS... |
| THE LIFELONG BENEFIT OF COMPLETING THIS COURSE IS... |
| AS A TRAINER HOW WILL I GO ABOUT ACHIEVING THESE GOALS? |
| WHAT WILL MAKE THIS COURSE A SUCCESS? |
| AS A TRAINER HOW WILL I FEEL IF I FAIL? |
| AS A TRAINER HOW WILL I FEEL IF I SUCCEED? |

# STEP 2: WRITING SUCCESS CRITERIA FOR EACH REVIEW ACTIVITY

Building review activities is not a difficult task. However, unless you have a clear outcome, the review may be touted as a time-filler, a 'fun' exercise with little or no point or, worse, a waste of time. Reviews need to be carefully thought through and, with a little planning, you will achieve your outcome and much more besides.

## CREATING SUCCESS CRITERIA FOR EACH REVIEW ACTIVITY

In order to get the true indicator of the success of your review activities, ensure that you establish the purpose or end goal when preparing the review activity. It is easy to write goals when you ask about specific activities: 'How will I know they know?' I refer to these review activity goals as success criteria. By reflecting on the success criteria for a review activity, you have a much better chance of knowing how successful you have been as a trainer and what your participants' chance of success will be when they go on to apply their skills in their workplace.

# STEP 3 (OPTIONAL): CREATING MULTI-LEVEL OBJECTIVES FROM HANDS-ON REVIEW ACTIVITIES

More experienced trainers may choose to build review activities with dual or triple goals. This means that while participants are completing the review activity they are reviewing a step-by-step process; however, participants can also be experiencing attitudinal change or be engaged in learning new or refining behaviours.

These secondary objectives are brought out during the debrief session of the review. The secondary objectives are debriefed only after the trainer is confident that participants have achieved the primary aim of reviewing the step-by-step procedure.

*Working example: customer service software training*
Take for example a course that trains a new software system for customer service employees. The review activity may start with creating a customer record in a new computer system. Half way through the activity, the trainer may interrupt the process and have the participants switch to a customer enquiry. After doing the enquiry, the participants return to create their original customer record. The trainer interrupts them again. This time the participants have to find details of a purchase order number that is in the system. After that, they come back a second time to finish the customer record. This simulation of day-to-day activity in the workplace is valuable.

This example shows how the activities review the content of three functions — creating a customer record, executing a customer enquiry and doing an enquiry on a purchase order number. It also illustrates the secondary objectives being taught — change, prioritising, quick thinking, patience and multi-tasking. These secondary objectives give the review activity depth and possibly provide a springboard into topics on those behaviours. As a trainer, you need to think through creating this type of review activity carefully, script your debrief questions to maximise learning and ensure participants are confident with their skills.

## SUMMARY

Each review activity should be evaluated against your success criteria. You can then decide whether it met your objectives, the objectives of your participants, the objectives of your content and the objectives of the organisation. If it fails in any or all of these areas, be ruthless — change it!

# CHAPTER FIVE

# LEVELS OF PARTICIPATION

* CREATING BALANCE THROUGH INVOLVEMENT

* PARTICIPATION LEVELS: FROM GROUPS TO INDIVIDUALS

* VARYING PARTICIPATION LEVELS DURING A COURSE

Review activities can assist you in creating an energetic learning environment that avoids the afternoon slump. With this in mind, your next decision is based on the amount of participation you want in the review activity. When designing courses more than two consecutive days in length, the need for active participation and involvement in teams becomes greater. This team approach keeps the spirit of the course alive and energetic. Review activities that are conducted by the participants as individuals can still be included during morning sessions and as overnight reviews. In fact, a mix of participation levels throughout the training course is required to accommodate the different learning preferences of individual participants and to balance energy levels throughout the training.

### PEOPLE GENERALLY WORK IN TEAMS OR WORKGROUPS

It is worth remembering that participants attending training courses rarely perform tasks in isolation in their real day-to-day working lives. In my experience, if participants are in sales, customer service, leadership and other types of 'people' job roles, they mainly enjoy working with others in team review activities. However, you will still need to ensure that there is a balance between the team and individual review activities to be conducted.

## CREATING AN ENVIRONMENT OF SELF-HELP

Technical courses are filled with process-driven information, and knowing how to be resourceful is part of the learning. Creating an environment of self-help for technical courses should be a priority for all technical trainers. Every day, people in the workplace summon resourcefulness to find the answers to their problems. Often non-hierarchical networks of people are created to meet these needs; sometimes a call is made to someone in an entirely different part of the organisation in order to short-circuit the traditional problem-solving methods. Emotional bonds and ties with participants on training courses are often realised as problem-solving relationships back in the workplace. If the trainer is aware of this, they can maximise this naturally occurring social mechanism — and the ideal place to do so is during the review activity process.

### HOW TO ENCOURAGE SELF-HELP AND RESOURCEFULNESS

In all technical review activities, I encourage participants to use any information they can in order to get the task done. Mostly, I encourage them to use any resource in the room, with the exception of me, their trainer. In regular training activities this is certainly not my approach, as I am there to help them as much or as little as they need — yet during review activities I encourage them not to use me as a resource. I tell them the reason they should try not to rely on me is that I will not always be next to them at their desks when they are at work — a reason they find to be valid. By this, they understand that they need to take responsibility for their learning, and not just rely on me to rescue them. Of course, during the review activity, if they are totally stuck I will provide clues to their next step, but rarely do I reveal exactly what they should do. This gives participants a sense of confidence.

Sometimes, I have attempted to help a participant during a review activity and the participant has said, 'No Catherine, don't help me, I want to see if I can do this.' Participants' confidence is boosted when they grasp a concept and can make it work for themselves.

Participants usually 'crib' from the flip charts around the room, the training material, on-line help, from each other, handouts and any other resource material they can find. This allows them to build informal networks of fellow participants who may become resources after the formal training has been completed.

### HOW EMOTIONAL INTELLIGENCE SUPPORTS THE NOTION OF SELF-HELP

In his book *Emotional Intelligence*, Daniel Goleman says, 'A [person] at Bell Labs talked about being stumped by a technical problem. He painstakingly called various technical gurus and then waited, wasting valuable time while calls went unreturned and email messages unanswered. When unexpected problems arise, the informal organisation kicks in. Its complex web of social ties forms every time colleagues communicate and solidifies over time into surprisingly stable networks. [These networks] skip entire functions to get things done.'

As a trainer, you can lay the foundation for this naturally occurring behaviour by allowing participants to use the collective intelligence of the group to get the task done.

# PARTICIPATION LEVELS: FROM WHOLE-GROUPS TO INDIVIDUALS

Trainers' skill levels, experience and confidence, along with the training objectives that have been set, will help to determine the participation level they favour.

## PARTICIPATION LEVEL 1: WHOLE GROUP REVIEW ACTIVITIES

Only a very confident and skilled trainer would be likely to choose to run a whole-group review activity. In a whole-group activity all the participants together are involved in a single task, not as separate teams or pairs. Whole-group sizes could range from six people to 600, or even more! These activities require careful facilitation to ensure that all participants are involved. Furthermore, a whole-group activity is more difficult to measure, because it is easier for quiet participants to blend in while more outgoing participants take the spotlight.

However, whole-group reviews work well when participants are like-minded and have similar personalities. They are often physically engaging, but they should include an individual-thinking component to incorporate all participants in the process.

Whole-group review activities are excellent when guided by the trainer, but often become unruly if left unsupervised. Problems arise when very dominant participants take over the process and railroad, bulldoze or even unconsciously threaten the retiring ones or deep thinkers in the group. I would recommend that whole group review activities be limited to group sizes that do not exceed 12 participants, or chaos may be the result!

## PARTICIPATION LEVEL 2: TEAM-BASED REVIEW ACTIVITIES

The ideal size of a team or group when conducting a review activity is five. Any more than five often means that dominant participants take over, leaving shy and reserved participants on the outside. Any fewer than three in a team activity and the sharing of information may become restrained because of the participants don't have enough ideas to work from within the group.

It is important for the trainer to supervise teams, taking note of what each participant is contributing. This can be done using the 'fly on the wall' approach. The trainer hovers in the background while listening closely to what is happening within each small group.

### CREATING A COMPETITIVE SPIRIT

Many trainers like to increase energy levels in a group by encouraging competition. Competition does not mean that you need to sacrifice learning or not achieve the success criteria of a review activity. Simple techniques, such as setting time limits and having teams race against the clock, are easy to employ.

Some of the review activities listed in this book create a competitive spirit as part of the activity. For example, Money Bags and Sale of the Minute create fierce competition: small teams aim to win as many points as possible by answering questions correctly.

Another way to increase energy through competition is to use a board game as a review activity. You can use commercially available board games and write questions relating to your course. Modify the rules if necessary. If you have the time and like to be creative you could create your own board game, invent questions and write some rules for play. Teams of four or five participants compete against each other to answer questions and move along the board towards the end. Along the way they collect points, 'cash' or objects in order to win the game.

### CREATING A SPIRIT OF ACCURACY AND CORRECTNESS

With many topics accuracy is the highest priority. For example, imagine you are training a credit management course for salespeople. The topic to be reviewed is the credit application form; specifically looking for errors and omissions when collecting the form from your customers. You may choose to conduct a review called the Eagle Eyes Review. To prepare for this review the trainer would complete a credit application form with numerous errors on it. The completed form would be given to small groups as a handout. Teams would be awarded points for the number of errors they find. This review rewards accuracy rather than speed while still generating team spirit and some competition.

You may choose to award small prizes to the winning team. It always amazes me how competitive adults will become when there is a prize at stake. I also award consolation prizes, so that everyone shares in the win.

Sometimes, when I am conducting a review activity I will be pleasantly surprised at an idea or way of applying new learning. Awards for inventiveness, creativity and resourcefulness might also be included. I use simple things like mini-chocolate bars or items bearing the company logo such as T-shirts or desk accessories.

## PARTICIPATION LEVEL 3: PAIR-AND-SHARE REVIEW ACTIVITIES

Pair-and-share reviews are excellent for promoting the sharing of information and are generally less active than team-based reviews. This style of cooperative review has become increasingly popular in training because of its excellent outcomes. Pair-and-share reviews foster close working relationships between participants and puts the trainer in a better position to measure the progress of each participant.

### A working example of pair and share

Imagine you are training a course in leadership, sales, quality or customer service with the communication topic of 'Inferences' in it. You have taught the definition and provided the synonyms: second-guessing, deduction, reason, judgment, supposition, implication and reading between the lines. Now, this is a difficult topic because participants are expected to think about their thinking and differentiating between what is actually observed and what is sometimes inferred is a sophisticated skill.

After teaching the topic you conduct an activity in which the whole group discusses the consequences of being unable to infer well. This is not a review activity because there is still new information being learnt. The outcome of that discussion is, first, a person might have difficulty in social settings because they are unable to 'read' other people. Second, a person might not see beyond the literal. Thirdly, a person might tend to take things at face value, without looking below the surface. Fourthly, a person might be easily taken in, because they miss the hidden agenda or the ulterior motives of others.

You have prepared a pair-and-share review activity. You give each group three frames of a movie, or picture. The pairs are then asked to list some of their observations. Based on these observations, the pairs make some inferences about the story. With the entire group you discuss the review activity to ensure that the key points from the discussion have been included in the review.

The second part of the topic is to teach the difference between observation and inference. Your key points include areas such as 'observations are low-level intellectual tasks', 'inferring requires the learner to search for meaning and to make sense of the observation' and 'finding the inference is a task of reflecting on the observations'.

You need to review this material and you do so using another pair-and-share review activity. Use the same pairs as before. This time you show a painting and the pairs write down first their observations, then their inferences. The pair are given a further five minutes to draw a rough 'before picture' and 'after picture' sketch to go with the painting they have been shown.

Before and after pictures are compared by the groups. The trainer ensures that during the explanation of their pictures, the pairs are accurately describing the theory of inferencing.

As a trainer, you need to be sure that this theory can be applied in the workplace. Again, the trainer uses a pair-and-share review where participants answer the question: How can we use the skill of inferencing in our day-to-day work? Participants create a list of ways they can apply this theory and share these with the whole group.

This is quite a complex example of a pair-and-share review activity. In fact, there are three pair-and-share review activities in this example. You can see that review activities can be slotted into a course, sometimes without the participant formally knowing they are reviewing. No announcement is necessary, the process takes care of itself. During the review activity the trainer is continuously gathering data to answer the question: At this end of this topic how do I know they know?

### ASSIGNING ROLES FOR A PAIR-AND-SHARE ACTIVITY

It is important that both participants in the activity work equally hard to complete the activity. Sometimes, if one participant is tending to dominate, you can assign roles for each member of the pair. For example, one person could be the 'input agent', doing the writing (or keyboard work on a computer course), and the other could be the 'resource agent', gathering information from resource material and 'cribbing' from other teams. This way you are sure that both participants are actively involved in the review activity.

Assigning roles can be done quickly and easily by asking the pair to choose one of the two identified roles. Another way to mix up the pairs and assign roles at the same time is to create regrouping cards. Using the input and resource example above, you would create enough cards for the whole group, half labelled 'input agent' and half labelled 'resource agent'. If a participant draws an input agent card they must find a resource agent and work with that person for the activity.

### 'I have an odd number of participants in my group!'

If you have an odd number of participants simply create a 'bonus resource agent' card. The person who draws the bonus card can join any team they like as a further resource agent. This way the person doesn't feel like the last person chosen for the team but, in fact, the most wanted person in the group!

## PARTICIPATION LEVEL 4: INDIVIDUAL REVIEW ACTIVITIES

Individual review activities are completed in the training room with free communication and interaction with other participants. It is only very rarely that I ask that 'no communication' should take place with other participants. This simulates a testing or examination environment, triggering memories of school and university for many participants — an environment totally unlike our usual work environments. I usually allow participants to interact with each other freely and encourage them to use any resource material they wish in order to complete the task.

The difference between setting an individual review and a metacognitive review (as follows) is in the design of the task. An individual review is a classic twist on questions and answers; true or false, short-answer statements presented in a non-examination environment. Metacognitive reviews are reflective by nature and focus on the application of the material learnt. They challenge participants to think about their thinking.

### MAXIMISING INDIVIDUAL REVIEW ACTIVITIES

The following are some suggestions for individual review activities. Use these freely and refer to the Chapter 8 in this book for further ideas.

- Set the individual review activity as an overnight task (such as crosswords, which are just 40 test questions disguised in a different format).
- Set a task to be completed away from the participant's desk, say a search for information through resource documents (such as journals, newspapers, reference books, etc.).
- Set hands-on computer activities that incorporate completing a series of 'checkpoint' questions at various points throughout the activity.
- Use competitions to encourage inventiveness and correctness (as opposed to first finished) that may run for the entire course, with points being awarded along the way.

## PARTICIPATION LEVEL 5: METACOGNITIVE REVIEW ACTIVITIES

Metacognitive or reflective reviews are vital, yet are very often overlooked. This style of review challenges participants, through structured activities, to be thinking about their thinking, and allows them to consider their application of learnt material. Metacognitive review activities also enable the participant to begin actively constructing meaning — making sense of the world by connecting new learning with what is already known. These are vital connections participants must make in order to apply their learning. It can happen either consciously or unconsciously but can be accelerated to the conscious level via review activities designed by the trainer.

The term 'metacognitive' is a training term that has a 'shades of grey' meaning, owing largely to the fact that it is used in a variety of contexts. The most commonly used shorthand definition of metacognition is accurate for our purposes: 'the act of thinking about thinking'. So as trainers we should invoke a spirit of allowing participants to reflect on their thinking. Professional trainers aim for participants to undergo genuine performance improvements. These performance improvements are not just about training, they are about a certain 'mental shift' that needs to occur via metacognitive reflection. The professional trainer must strive for genuine performance improvements as a minimum expectation. Not to expect this is simply not doing a responsible training job.

Often, during a training session, participants tend to see things at face value, without looking beneath the surface. They are enveloped in their observations of the content, other participants and the trainer, which are all low-level intellectual tasks. Allowing time in a training room for participants to ponder, reason and deliberate over the work learnt further improves the odds on the material being applied.

Metacognitive review activities require the participant to search for meaning and to make sense of their observations, that is undertake the metacognitive task of reflecting on their observations. These review activities are always conducted on an individual basis and not necessarily always shared with the rest of the group.

### SUGGESTED METACOGNITIVE REVIEW ACTIVITIES

What follows are some suggestions for metacognitive review activities. Reference can also be had to Chapter 8. The good news for trainers is that because metacognitive review activities are 'thinking' activities, they involve very little preparation!

- The trainer uses a flip chart or handout to write reflective questions, trigger words or open-ended statements. Participants then carry out the task of answering questions, writing down what is triggered in their mind or completing the open-ended statement. This is done individually and, if appropriate, shared with a partner or the rest of the group.
- A variation on this theme is to have participants write a postcard from the course to themselves expressing their reflections on a part of the content or the course to date. The trainer would post the postcard to the participants after the course.
- Participants can be given learning journals in which to write down key points learnt. They should also note how they would apply their learning in their workplace.
- A 'hot tips' sheet can be created for participants on which to record their top 10 key points learnt in a training session, training day or the whole course. An extension of this activity is 'Ad campaign' (see Chapter 8).

# VARYING PARTICIPATION LEVELS DURING A COURSE

A mix of different training review activities not only provides variety for the participants and the trainer but, most important, provides participants with different ways of learning.

## CREATING BALANCE IN PARTICIPATION LEVELS DURING A COURSE

The following serves as an example of how to schedule a mix of review activities across a classic three-day training course and of how little training time it takes to run them. This example is not based on any particular content, type of participant or organisation. Rather it is a template and guide on which you can base your own mix of training. I have used the standard training day, starting at 8.30 a.m. and finishing at 5.00 p.m. If the training day is longer, adjust the model as necessary.

I have added levels of participation to the three-days-plus model of course development given in the previous chapter. This model serves as a guide only and is given to show how balance can be achieved. You can adapt this broad strategy to accommodate all course durations.

**FIGURE 5.1** // TYPES OF REVIEW ACTIVITIES

MODEL OF A SAMPLE TRAINING COURSE SHOWING PLACEMENT OF REVIEW ACTIVITIES

| TIME OF DAY 8.30 A.M. –5.00 P.M. | DAY 1 | TOTAL REVIEW TIME | DAY 2, 3, 4, ETC. (REPEAT EACH DAY) | TOTAL REVIEW TIME | LAST TRAINING DAY | TOTAL REVIEW TIME |
|---|---|---|---|---|---|---|
| 8.30 –10.00 (90 MINS) | | | START OF DAY REVIEW (30 MINS) • WHOLE GROUP WITH METACOGNITIVE ELEMENT | 30 | START OF DAY REVIEW (30 MINS) • SMALL GROUP | 30 |
| 10.00–10.15 | BREAK | | BREAK | | BREAK | |
| 10.15–11 (65 MINS) | START OF SESSION REVIEW (5 MINS) • PAIR AND SHARE END OF SESSION REVIEW (5 MINS) • SMALL GROUP | 10 | START OF SESSION REVIEW (5 MINS) • METACOGNITIVE END OF SESSION REVIEW (5 MINS) • SMALL GROUP | 10 | START OF SESSION REVIEW (5 MINS) • METACOGNITIVE END OF SESSION REVIEW (5 MINS) • PAIR AND SHARE | 10 |
| 11.20 –11.30 | BREAK | | BREAK | | BREAK | |
| 11.30 –12.30 (65 MINS) | START OF SESSION REVIEW (5 MINS) • METACOGNITIVE END OF SESSION REVIEW (5 MINS) • PAIR AND SHARE | 10 | START OF SESSION REVIEW (5 MINS) • PAIR AND SHARE END OF SESSION REVIEW (5 MINS) • SMALL GROUP | 10 | START OF SESSION REVIEW (5 MINS) • METACOGNITIVE END OF SESSION REVIEW (5 MINS) • PAIR AND SHARE | 10 |
| 12.30 –1.30. | LUNCH BREAK | 0 | LUNCH BREAK | 0 | LUNCH BREAK | 0 |
| 1.30–2.30 (60 MINS) | POST LUNCH REVIEW (15 MINS) • WHOLE GROUP END OF SESSION REVIEW (5 MINS) • SMALL GROUP | 20 | POST LUNCH REVIEW (15 MINS) • WHOLE GROUP OR SMALL GROUP (TEAM COMPETITION) END OF SESSION REVIEW (5 MINS) • PAIR AND SHARE | 20 | POST LUNCH REVIEW (15 MINS) • WHOLE GROUP END OF SESSION REVIEW (5 MINS) • SMALL GROUP | 20 |
| 2.30 –2.45 | BREAK (15 MINS) | 0 | BREAK | 0 | BREAK | 0 |
| 2.45 –3.45 (60 MINS) | START OF SESSION REVIEW (5 MINS) • METACOGNITIVE END OF SESSION REVIEW (5 MINS) • INDIVIDUAL | 10 | START OF SESSION REVIEW (5 MINS) • METACOGNITIVE END OF SESSION REVIEW (5 MINS) • PAIR AND SHARE | 10 | START OF SESSION REVIEW (5 MINS) • METACOGNITIVE END OF SESSION REVIEW (5 MINS) • INDIVIDUAL | 10 |
| 3.45 –3.55 | BREAK (10 MINS) | 0 | BREAK | 0 | BREAK | 0 |
| (65 MINS) | END OF DAY REVIEW (30 MINS) • SMALL GROUP (TEAM COMPETITION) SET OVERNIGHT REVIEW TASK (5 MINS) • METACOGNITIVE OR INDIVIDUAL | 35 | END OF DAY REVIEW (30 MINS) • SMALL GROUP (TEAM COMPETITION) SET OVERNIGHT REVIEW TASK (5 MINS) • METACOGNITIVE OR INDIVIDUAL | 35 | END OF DAY REVIEW (30 MINS) • SMALL GROUP (TEAM COMPETITION) SET OVERNIGHT REVIEW TASK (5 MINS) | 45 |
| TIME IN MINUTES SPENT REVIEWING: | TOTAL DAY 1 (1 HOUR 30 MINS) | 85 | TOTAL DAY 2, 3, 4, ETC. (2 HOURS 20 MINS) | 115 | TOTAL LAST DAY (2 HOURS 25 MINS) | 125 |

## SUMMARY

A training course needs a balanced approach to levels of participation. A mix of participation levels throughout the training course is required to accommodate the preferences of individual participants and to maintain the balance of energy throughout the duration of the training. Creating an environment of self-help for technical courses is of paramount importance and should be a priority for all technical trainers.

- A whole group activity is when the participants are involved in one task as the entire group, not as separate teams or pairs. It requires careful facilitation to ensure that all participants are involved.
- The ideal size of a team or group for conducting a review activity is five. Any more than five often means that dominant participants take over, leaving shy and reserved participants on the outside.
- Pair-and-share reviews are excellent at promoting sharing of information and are generally less active than team-based reviews. This style of cooperative review has become increasingly popular in training because of its excellent outcomes.
- Individual review activities are completed in the training room with free communication and interaction with other participants. If you don't allow participants to communicate freely with others, they often feel like they are in a test or exam environment, which, for many adult learners, can stall the learning process altogether.
- Metacognitive review activities enable the participant to begin actively constructing meaning, that is making sense of the world by connecting new learning with what is already known.

# CHAPTER SIX

# UNDERSTANDING DIFFERENT NEEDS OF PARTICIPANTS

* ASSUMPTIONS WE MAKE ABOUT ADULT LEARNING

* TWO WAYS TO CREATE BALANCE FOR ADULT LEARNERS

* USING MULTIPLE INTELLIGENCE TO CREATE BALANCE

Much has been written about the different needs and learning styles of individual participants during a training course. It is clear from the results of this research that there are many different theoretical models from which we can infer our own personal and preferred learning style. Your participants are individuals, so your choice of review methods needs to be varied and designed to meet those individual needs. This chapter aims to assist you with choosing and mixing review activities to meet the needs of different participants and these pages also provide guidelines for scheduling reviews in a typical three-day training course.

## ASSUMPTIONS MADE ABOUT ADULT LEARNERS

As a trainer, I can't hope to fully identify and understand the complex learning styles of each participant in my training room. Even if I could, there are certain assumptions that I must make prior to the course, otherwise I would still be doing instructional design while training! Even though I modify the training course while it's happening, all of my preparation is completed well before the training day, with contingency plans built in and little left to chance.

The following list is a snapshot of assumptions that professional trainers often make about their adult participants. It is not intended to be complete, but can be used as a guide for creating a review activity. These assumptions drive the thinking of the instructional designer whose aim it is to create a balanced and varied training program with a variety of review activities that suit most of the participants, most of the time. As trainers we often assume that all adult learners

- strive to be more competent, skilled and knowledgeable
- have the capacity to learn and want to do so
- will schedule time to apply the new learning to their day-to-day work
- will practise a new task to gain confidence with it, because they need to
- prefer non-threatening learning environments, where mistakes are viewed as learning opportunities
- bring to the training course their experiences at other training courses they have attended as adult learners.

We often also assume that some adult learners
- change their minds about how they wish to take in new information (often without notice), while others consistently take in new information in their preferred way
- happily work in teams while others enjoy working alone or would prefer to work with one other person
- only really understand the new content after a period of time has elapsed (say

overnight) when they have had time to reflect on the material, while others are quick to know how they will apply their learning on the job or in their lives

- would prefer to work with like-minded people, while others benefit from working with people totally different from themselves
- like competition, while others dislike competition
- consider a balance between having fun in a training room and spending time learning new things to be productive, while others prefer a strict learning environment where 'fun' has no place
- enjoy being tested and extended, while others like to 'cheat' using all the available resources around them, including reference material, other people, training aids or their own notes
- love working on hands-on project activities, while others prefer lecture-style training
- enjoy taking notes, while others prefer to be given their notes
- enjoy taking notes using coloured markers, while others prefer to write with a black or blue pen
- participate actively in discussions, while others prefer to work alone and reflect on what they have learnt
- and so on...and so forth.

These assumptions could fill an entire book. It is apparent that when we assume things of other adults, their behaviour and our expectations about their learning, we are often totally incorrect!

It is impossible to know the exact mix of preferences for each individual participant. Each individual brings to the training room a lifetime of experience, thousands of hours in a classroom environment and the capacity to change their mind quicker than you can keep up!

Where does all this leave you, the professional trainer?

## YOUR ONLY OPTION: ADOPT A BALANCED APPROACH

A balanced approach means that different styles of training are presented at different times throughout the course. This mix could include mini-lectures and activities conducted for the whole group, small teams, pairs and individuals. The mix could also include visual, auditory, kinesthetic and metacognitive (reflective) activities. It could cater for the different types of intelligence as described by Howard Gardner. This mix would extend with both learning and review activities.

So that you adopt a balanced approach when choosing a mix of review activities, remember the assumptions listed above. One thing should remain uppermost in your mind: how YOU learn as the trainer is not important. You need to accommodate all types of learners, who may or may not learn in the same way as you.

# CREATING BALANCE IN TWO WAYS

This book is not intended to be about adult learning style, but it is worth mentioning at this point that there are two simple ways to create balance using theories that have been used by trainers for some years.

One way to create balance is by using the straightforward theory of adult learning styles, involving visual, auditory and kinesthetic (VAK) issues. The second way to create balance is via Howard Gardner's theory of multiple intelligence. Other learning style models may be used to create balance, for example Bernice McCarthy's 4-Mat system, the theory of global and specific learners and many others.*

To ensure simplicity and a first base for learning, it is worthwhile exploring how VAK and multiple intelligence can be used when designing review activities.

## USING THE VAK LEARNING STYLES TO CREATE BALANCE

Countless publications and books refer to the adult learning styles based on sensory intake of information. Many trainers now accept that adults learn primarily by taking in information through the five senses — hearing, sight, taste, touch and smell. It is also widely accepted that three of these predominate for most training courses, namely visual (sight), auditory (hearing) and kinesthetic (touch and physical movement).

Many professional trainers ensure that their training courses accommodate all three senses. To this end, the trainer ensures that, first, auditory learners are accommodated by the inclusion of mini-lectures, discussions and music. Second, visual learners are accommodated by visual aids: the trainer may use flip charts, provide coloured markers with which to take notes, use handouts, video, overheads and so on. Thirdly, trainers accommodate the needs of a kinesthetic learner by group work, hands-on activities and physical movement. In this way, balance is created during content and activity sessions.

Similarly, review activities also can be balanced for to visual, auditory and kinesthetic learning styles. This balance is introduced during the development stages of the course, with the focus not just on a single review activity but an entire training course. The combination of review activities thus accommodates the needs of visual, auditory and kinesthetic learners.

If this kind of balance is not struck, participants may be unfairly advantaged or disadvantaged. For example, a trainer who lectures will appeal to auditory learners, and they will probably learn faster than others who may not only struggle to stay focused but will have to work harder to understand and assimilate the learning.

### EXAMPLES OF HOW TO CREATE BALANCE USING VAK

The following table explains some ways of incorporating VAK across the training course to provide balance:

---

* If you are new to this theory may I suggest you begin your exploration of it by reading Gardner's book *Frames of Mind*. This and Gardner's other books will help you to enhance your understanding of the multiple intelligence theory and your investment in reading time should certainly pay off handsomely in your training.

| STYLE OF LEARNER | INCLUSIONS IN REVIEW ACTIVITIES THAT SUPPORT LEARNING STYLE |
|---|---|
| VISUAL | • SPOT-THE-ERROR ACTIVITIES, WHERE PARTICIPANTS HAVE TO LOOK FOR ERRORS IN A CASE STUDY, HANDOUT OR OTHER WRITTEN MATERIAL.<br>• GENERAL USE OF COLOUR AND PICTURES, E.G. CARDS WITH TRUE OR FALSE STATEMENTS, FILL-IN-THE-GAPS HANDOUTS, FLIP CHARTS WITH WELL ILLUSTRATED REVIEW ACTIVITIES.<br>• PUZZLES IN WHICH THE FINAL PICTURE COMPLETES A STEP-BY-STEP PROCESS. |
| AUDITORY | • TELLING OTHERS WHAT THEY HAVE LEARNT.<br>• LISTENING TO AN AUDIO CASSETTE OR VIDEO AS A CASE STUDY.<br>• LISTENING TO 'HOT TIPS' FROM OTHER PARTICIPANTS.<br>• RHYTHMIC LEARNING TO LEARN KEY CONCEPTS OR A SERIES OF STEPS IN A PROCESS. |
| KINESTHETIC | • PHYSICALLY SORTING CARDS INTO DIFFERENT CATEGORIES (E.G. TRUE/FALSE, TERM/DEFINITION AND SO ON)<br>• BOARD GAMES IN WHICH TEAMS COMPETE.<br>• PUZZLES AND JIGSAWS, IN WHICH PARTICIPANTS CAN BE ACTIVELY INVOLVED.<br>• USE OF ROLE-PLAY AS A SKILL PRACTICE (THIS DOESN'T MEAN IN FRONT OF THE WHOLE GROUP. REMEMBER THAT SOME KINESTHETIC LEARNERS ARE STILL SHY OR UNCERTAIN!). |

# USING MULTIPLE INTELLIGENCE TO CREATE BALANCE

Howard Gardner and his theory of each person having distinct styles of intelligence has been widely accepted by educators. Gardner's theory is used in schools and in adult education.

The intelligences identified by Gardner are visual, auditory, kinesthetic, mathematical/ logical, musical, linguistic, interpersonal and intrapersonal. Some alignment can be made between visual and kinesthetic intelligence as described by Gardner and the VAK theory as discussed above. Let's have a brief look at the other intelligences. They are largely self-explanatory.

### MATHEMATICAL/LOGICAL INTELLIGENCE

Mathematical/logical intelligence is found in people who find steps, sequences and the processes of mathematics straightforward. In technical or process training, steps and sequences form much of what is to be remembered. Focusing review activities on step-by-step actions assists this process.

### MUSICAL INTELLIGENCE

People with musical intelligence respond well not only to music but also to rhythmic learning. I remember a classmate at school who used to put the key points of a lesson into a rhyme or rhythm to assist with memorising them for exams. Today, as a trainer, I use this technique as a review mechanism. Having started playing the piano at 10 years of age, I find it simple to put key learning points into a rhythm. If this process is not as easy for you, your participants will generally delight in having the opportunity to compose their own rhythms, which will anchor the learnings for them. I suggest that small groups be assigned the task of choosing their own key learning points and then composing a rhythm. Having the groups 'perform' their composition helps to further reinforce the learning.

### LINGUISTIC INTELLIGENCE

Gardner describes linguistic intelligence as being higher in people who absorb new material through language, that is listening to the spoken word, talking, reading or writing. Review activities that are centred on reading, discussion or listening will support linguistic intelligence.

### INTERPERSONAL AND INTRAPERSONAL INTELLIGENCE

Interpersonal intelligence is high when learners enjoy group learning situations in which new material can be shared and discussed with others. Those who would rather learn alone and or require reflective time to extract meaning from the new material as it relates to their own lives prefer intrapersonal intelligence. A mix of review activities will meet the needs of both styles of learners.

## EXAMPLES OF HOW TO CREATE BALANCE USING THE SEVEN INTELLIGENCES

The following table provides a springboard for creating balance. It is not intended to be a complete listing of options to maximise the intelligences, just an introductory guide.

**FIGURE 6.2** // CREATING BALANCE USING THE SEVEN INTELLIGENCES

| STYLE OF LEARNER | INCLUSIONS IN REVIEW ACTIVITIES THAT SUPPORT THE LEARNING STYLE |
| --- | --- |
| VISUAL | • REFER TO THE VAK TABLE ABOVE. |
| KINESTHETIC | • REFER TO THE VAK TABLE ABOVE. |
| MATHEMATICAL /LOGICAL | • JUMBLES OF SEQUENCES TO PUT BACK IN ORDER.<br>• FOCUS ON STEP-BY-STEP PROCEDURES.<br>• EXAMINE WHY STEPS ARE RANGED IN A PARTICULAR SEQUENCE AND CREATE 'WHAT IF' SCENARIOS. |
| MUSICAL | • CREATE A RHYTHM, RHYME OR SONG ABOUT KEY POINTS IN THE TOPIC.<br>• CREATE A RHYMING VERSE FROM KEY POINTS IN THE TOPIC.<br>• USE MUSIC TO CREATE A RELAXED LEARNING ENVIRONMENT —USE ONLY DURING ACTIVITIES, REVIEW ACTIVITIES, BREAKS AND INDIVIDUAL REFLECTION, NOT DURING MINI-LECTURES. |
| LINGUISTIC | • WRITE A STORY USING TERMS FROM THE TOPIC TAUGHT AND READ THE STORIES ALOUD TO THE GROUP.<br>• PROVIDE WRITTEN WORK THAT PARTICIPANTS MUST ANALYSE.<br>• CREATE FILL-IN-THE-GAPS HANDOUTS.<br>• CREATE CROSSWORD PUZZLES (DISGUISE 40–50 TEST QUESTIONS AS AN ENJOYABLE REVIEW ACTIVITY). |
| INTERPERSONAL | • HOLD GROUP DISCUSSIONS, GUIDED OR SEMI-GUIDED BY THE TRAINER.<br>• CREATE OPPORTUNITIES FOR PARTICIPANTS TO SHARE THEIR LEARNINGS.<br>• USE BOARD GAMES AND OTHER TEAM ACTIVITIES TO ENGAGE INTERPERSONAL SKILLS.<br>• USE PARTICIPANTS' OWN EXPERIENCES TO REVIEW AND SUPPORT LEARNING POINTS. |
| INTRAPERSONAL | • CREATE 'QUIET TIME' OPPORTUNITIES FOR PARTICIPANTS TO THINK ABOUT THEIR THINKING.<br>• PROVIDE INDIVIDUAL, REFLECTIVE REVIEW ACTIVITIES LIKE 'WAYS IN WHICH I CAN APPLY MY LEARNING'.<br>• HAVE PARTICIPANTS CREATE AN 'EMOTIONAL INTELLIGENCE NETWORK CHART' ON WHERE THEY CAN GET SUPPORT AND HELP IN APPLYING THEIR LEARNING.<br>• PROVIDE PARTICIPANTS WITH A LEARNING JOURNAL, WHERE THEY RECORD WHAT THEY HAVE LEARNT AND HOW THEY CAN APPLY IT. |

## ACCOMMODATING SEVERAL LEARNING STYLES AT ONCE
### *Working case study: Negotiation skills*

Always remember that most review activities support several learning styles at once. Imagine you are training a course on negotiation skills and have decided to have a lively review activity immediately following lunch. You decide to use a crossword puzzle. Immediately we know that a crossword puzzle is aimed at the linguistic learner; however, with some simple changes many other styles can be accommodated as well. Some of these changes include

- enlarging the A4-size crossword into two flip-chart-size crossword puzzles and mounting them on the wall
- providing each participant with a clue sheet
- creating two teams which race each other to complete their own giant team crossword puzzles.

These changes have now broadened the appeal to include kinesthetic and interpersonal learners (team-based crossword) and visual learners (giant poster-size crosswords).

### ACCOMMODATING OTHER INTELLIGENCES

With an alternative twist, the negotiation skills crossword puzzle, while still suiting linguistic learners, will also accommodate the intrapersonal learner. Instead of using the crossword puzzle as a lively post-lunch review activity, you can decide to use it as an overnight review.

- You print the blank crossword puzzle and the clues as a handout and have participants complete it on the first evening of the course.
- Participants complete the crossword either at home that evening or before the course starts the following day.

### GETTING BETTER AT USING THE SEVEN INTELLIGENCES

During a recent visit to Australia, Howard Gardner held a conference on the theory of multiple intelligence. His dry sense of humour and amazing mind kept all of the 1000 delegates alert for two days. One interesting task that he set during the conference was to redesign a single training session to use all of the intelligences. Since that conference, many trainers have used train-the-trainer or in-service training days to try out this instructional design activity.

Going back to our negotiation skills training example, you might choose 'Preparing for the negotiation' as your single topic redesign opportunity from the two-day training course.

Trainers are challenged to rewrite the session using all seven intelligences, with one proviso — the final duration of the session must not exceed the original time taken to train the topic (in this case, preparing for the negotiation takes 45 minutes to train).

This exercise is an outstanding way for a group of trainers to increase their knowledge of Gardner's theory and hone their instructional design and creativity skills. Any topic can be used for this train-the-trainer activity. Start with a simple 50-minute session and recreate it using as many of the intelligences as possible. Then expand the activity and redesign a one-day or two-day training course. You will be amazed at the effective and creative result!

## SUMMARY

Using a combination of learning style theories creates balance in review activities. The two learning style examples are VAK and Gardner's multiple intelligences. Most instructional designers would agree that using a mix of learning styles is the most basic consideration when creating a training course. Sadly though, many still create training courses that support styles of learning that suit their own personal preferences, without considering participants' own styles.

Instructional designers, course developers and trainers who do provide balance give their training courses the structure and mechanisms that raise the odds of keeping all participants focused throughout the course and learning according to their preferred style. As you can see from the negotiation skills example, it is quite straightforward to add balance to a training day by using a variety of review activities.

# CHAPTER SEVEN

# DAILY PLANS AND THE ROLE OF THE TRAINER

* THE ROLE OF THE TRAINER DURING THE REVIEW ACTIVITY

* REVIEW FOR ITS OWN SAKE?

* HAVING GENUINE INTEREST IN YOUR PARTICIPANTS

# MAINTAINING THE BALANCE — NEW VERSUS REVIEW

Juggling training time between delivering new content and checking learning is one of the most complex balancing acts in the training profession. A trainer must regulate the amount of new information being delivered to participants, while ensuring that participants are absorbing this information and are ready to apply it back at the workplace. For some more fortunate trainers, this juggling act comes naturally. They simply know or sense when their participants are overloaded, ready to move on or travelling okay.

The skill of juggling new versus review might come with extensive training experience or simply as an innate ability. But, for many trainers, it is a case of unconscious incompetence, or not knowing what they don't know. These trainers are unaware that they should be concerned with keeping this balance and so blindly continue to pump out new information. Most new and even some seasoned trainers — when their incompetence becomes conscious — need guidance and instruction on how to strike this balance.

If the balance is not maintained between delivering new information and checking existing knowledge, the training degenerates into one of two scenarios. The first is when the training becomes something of a roller-coaster ride and the trainer does not check whether the participants are actually learning anything. The second scenario is the reverse. The training is hinged excessively on review activities with the participants having to go over and over the same material, resulting in disengagement or, worse, boredom. Once mastered, the skill of maintaining the balance provides rich rewards. Participants develop a healthy enthusiasm for learning, are never overwhelmed and maintain their confidence in the training room.

# THE MODELS IN THIS CHAPTER

This chapter will help you to manage this juggling act so that you can strike a balance between the time taken to train new material and the time taken to review. Use these models freely to assist you when developing your training courses. These templates are effective for HRD, non-technical and technical courses alike. They are the basis of my running sheets. A running sheet (or session plan) gives me a snapshot of exactly what will be happening in my training course — both the content to be delivered and the process by which it will be delivered. From the running sheet, I develop a trainer's guide and the participant handouts.

When you've looked at the models provided, read the second part of this chapter carefully. It examines the role of the trainer during a review activity.

### THE MODEL FOR HALF-DAY TRAINING COURSES
The first model shows a three-hour training course, starting at 8.30 a.m. and finishing at 12.00 midday. This model can easily be adapted for an afternoon or evening session.

**FIGURE 7.1** // HALF-DAY TRAINING COURSE MODEL

| TIME OF DAY 8.30 A.M.–12.00 P.M. | HALF-DAY TRAINING COURSE | TOTAL REVIEW TIME |
|---|---|---|
| 8.30 –10.00 (90 MINUTES) | OPENING SESSION<br>• OPENING (20 MINUTES)<br>• TRAINING (70 MINUTES) | 0 |
| 10.00 –10.15 | BREAK 15 MINUTES | |
| 10.15 –11.05 (65 MINUTES) | • START OF SESSION REVIEW (5 MINUTES)<br>• TRAINING (45 MINUTES)<br>• END OF SESSION REVIEW (5 MINUTES) | 5<br><br>5 |
| 10 11.05 –11.15 | MINI-BREAK 10 MINUTES | |
| 11.15 –12.00 (65 MINUTES) | • TRAINING (15 MINUTES)<br>• END OF COURSE REVIEW (15 MINUTES)<br>• SUMMARY, EVALUATION AND CLOSE (15 MINUTES) | <br>15 |
| 12.00 | END OF COURSE | |
| TOTAL REVIEW TIME IN HALF-DAY DAY TRAINING COURSE | | 25 MINUTES |

## THE MODEL FOR ONE-DAY TRAINING COURSES

The sample one-day training course begins at 8.30 a.m. and finishes at 5.00 p.m. It builds on the half-day model. The post-lunch review is vital for refocusing participants and will assist with overcoming the post-lunch blues. (I refer to this time of the day as teflon hour: when nothing sticks!) This review should be kinesthetic, with high involvement from participants.

**FIGURE 7.2** // ONE-DAY TRAINING COURSE MODEL

| TIME OF DAY 8.30 A.M.–5.00 P.M. | ONE-DAY TRAINING COURSE | TOTAL REVIEW TIME |
|---|---|---|
| 8.30–10.00 (90 MINUTES) | OPENING SESSION:<br>• OPENING (20 MINUTES)<br>• TRAINING (70 MINUTES) | 0 |
| 10.00–10.15 | BREAK 15 MINUTES | |
| 10.15–11.15 (60 MINUTES) | • START OF SESSION REVIEW (5 MINUTES)<br>• TRAINING (45 MINUTES)<br>• END OF SESSION REVIEW (5 MINUTES) | 5<br><br>5 |
| 10 11.15–11.30 | BREAK 15 MINUTES | |
| 11.30–12.30 (60 MINUTES) | • START OF SESSION REVIEW (5 MINUTES)<br>• TRAINING (50 MINUTES)<br>• END OF SESSION REVIEW (5 MINUTES) | 5<br><br>5 |
| 12.30–1.30 | LUNCH 60 MINUTES | |
| 1.30–2.30 (60 MINUTES) | • POST-LUNCH REVIEW (15 MINUTES)<br>• TRAINING (45 MINUTES) | 15 |
| 2.30–2.45 | BREAK 15 MINUTES | |
| 2.45–3.45 (60 MINUTES) | • START OF SESSION REVIEW (5 MINUTES)<br>• TRAINING (50 MINUTES)<br>• END OF SESSION REVIEW (5 MINUTES) | 5<br><br>5 |
| 3.45–3.55 | BREAK 10 MINUTES | |
| 3.55–5.00 (65 MINUTES) | • TRAINING (20 MINUTES)<br>• END OF DAY REVIEW (30 MINUTES)<br>• SUMMARY, EVALUATION AND CLOSE (15 MINUTES) | <br>30 |
| 5.00 | END OF COURSE | |
| TOTAL REVIEW TIME IN ONE-DAY TRAINING COURSE | | 75 MINUTES |

## THE MODEL FOR TWO-DAY TRAINING COURSES

You will notice below that the total time for review increases on the second training day. This is because of the process of building knowledge. The review on the morning of Day 2 covers the 'must know' content from Day 1. Then, throughout Day 2, each review continues to build on the content. For example, start of session review activities not only review content from the previous session, but also the content from the sessions before that. This way, the participants continuously build their knowledge and the trainer has an opportunity to ensure that each participant is properly conversant with the important messages in the course so far.

Another vital factor in the two-day training course (or any multi-day training course) is the start-of-day review on the morning of Day 2. This major review covers all the important elements of content delivered on Day 1. It is an opportunity for the trainer to assess whether or not the participants are confident with the Day 1 material. For the participants, the start-of-day review helps to refocus them on their Day 1 learnings and begins the important process of building their confidence with their new skills and knowledge and the metacognitive process of deciding how they will apply these learnings in their lives.

**FIGURE 7.3** // TWO-DAY TRAINING COURSE MODEL

| TIME OF DAY 8.30 A.M. –5.00 P.M. | DAY 1 | TOTAL REVIEW TIME | DAY 2 | TOTAL REVIEW TIME |
|---|---|---|---|---|
| 8.30–10.00 (90 MINUTES) | OPENING SESSION<br>• OPENING (20 MINUTES)<br>• TRAINING (70 MINUTES) | 0 | OPENING SESSION<br>• START OF DAY REVIEW (30 MINUTES)<br>• TRAINING (50 MINUTES) | 30 |
| 10.00–10.15 | BREAK 15 MINUTES | | BREAK 15 MINUTES | |
| 10.15–11.15 (60 MINUTES) | • START OF SESSION REVIEW (5 MINUTES)<br>• TRAINING (45 MINUTES)<br>• END OF SESSION REVIEW (5 MINUTES) | 5<br><br>5 | • START OF SESSION REVIEW (5 MINUTES)<br>• TRAINING (45 MINUTES)<br>• END OF SESSION REVIEW (5 MINUTES) | 5<br><br>5 |
| 11.15–11.30 | BREAK 15 MINUTES | | BREAK 15 MINUTES | |
| 11.30–12.30 (60 MINUTES) | • START OF SESSION REVIEW (5 MINUTES)<br>• TRAINING (50 MINUTES)<br>• END OF SESSION REVIEW | 5<br><br>5 | • START OF SESSION REVIEW (5 MINUTES)<br>• TRAINING (50 MINUTES)<br>• END OF SESSION REVIEW (5 MINUTES) | 5<br><br>5 |
| 12.30–1.30 | LUNCH 60 MINUTES | | LUNCH 60 MINUTES | |
| 1.30–2.30 (60 MINUTES) | • POST-LUNCH REVIEW (15 MINUTES)<br>• TRAINING (40 MINUTES)<br>• END OF SESSION REVIEW (5 MINUTES) | 15<br><br>5 | • POST-LUNCH REVIEW (15 MINUTES)<br>• TRAINING (40 MINUTES)<br>• END OF SESSION REVIEW (5 MINUTES) | 15<br><br>5 |
| 2.30–2.45 | BREAK 15 MINUTES | | BREAK 15 MINUTES | |
| 2.45–3.45 (60 MINUTES) | • START OF SESSION REVIEW (5 MINUTES)<br>• TRAINING (50 MINUTES)<br>• END OF SESSION REVIEW (5 MINUTES) | 5<br><br>5 | • START OF SESSION REVIEW (5 MINUTES)<br>• TRAINING (50 MINUTES)<br>• END OF SESSION REVIEW (5 MINUTES) | 5<br><br>5 |
| 3.45–3.55 | BREAK 10 MINUTES | | BREAK 10 MINUTES | |
| 3.55–5.00 (65 MINUTES) | • TRAINING (25 MINUTES)<br>• END OF DAY REVIEW (30 MINUTES)<br>• SET OVERNIGHT REVIEW TASK (5 MINUTES)<br>• SUMMARY AND CLOSE (5 MINUTES) | 30<br>5 | • TRAINING (20 MINUTES)<br>• END OF DAY REVIEW (30 MINUTES)<br>• SUMMARY, EVALUATION AND CLOSE (15 MINUTES) | 30 |
| 5.00 P.M. | END OF COURSE | | END OF COURSE | |
| | TOTAL REVIEW TIME ON DAY1 85 MINUTES | | TOTAL REVIEW TIME ON DAY 2 110 MINUTES | |

# THE MODEL FOR THREE-DAY TRAINING COURSES

As courses get longer participants' and trainers' energy levels decline! Participants need to stop, reflect, pause and review what they have learnt.

Whether or not the three days are split up, the following model will make it possible for trainers to know that their participants know, and give them much needed time to review what they have learnt, thereby building the confidence to learn more.

**FIGURE 7.4** // THREE-DAY TRAINING COURSE MODEL
THREE-DAY TRAINING COURSE (DAYS CONSECUTIVE OR SPLIT UP) TIME OF DAY

| TIME OF DAY 8.30 A.M.–5.00 P.M. | DAY 1 | TOTAL REVIEW TIME | DAY 2 | TOTAL REVIEW TIME | DAY 3 | TOTAL REVIEW TIME |
|---|---|---|---|---|---|---|
| 8.30–10.00 A.M. (90 MINUTES) | OPENING SESSION<br>• OPENING (20 MINUTES)<br>• TRAINING (70 MINUTES) | 0 | OPENING SESSION<br>• START OF DAY REVIEW (30 MINUTES)<br>• TRAINING (50 MINUTES) | 30 | OPENING SESSION<br>• START OF DAY REVIEW (30 MINUTES)<br>• TRAINING (50 MINUTES) | 30 |
| 10.00–10.15 | BREAK 15 MINUTES | | BREAK 15 MINUTES | | BREAK 15 MINUTES | |
| 10.15–11.15 (60 MINUTES) | • START OF SESSION REVIEW (5 MINUTES)<br>• TRAINING (45 MINUTES)<br>• END OF SESSION REVIEW (5 MINUTES) | 5<br><br>5 | • START OF SESSION REVIEW (5 MINUTES)<br>• TRAINING (45 MINUTES)<br>• END OF SESSION REVIEW (5 MINUTES) | 10 | • START OF SESSION REVIEW (5 MINUTES)<br>• TRAINING (45 MINUTES)<br>• END OF SESSION REVIEW (5 MINUTES) | 5<br><br>5 |
| 11.15–11.30 | BREAK 15 MINUTES | | BREAK 15 MINUTES | | BREAK 15 MINUTES | |
| 11.30–12.30 (60 MINUTES) | • START OF SESSION REVIEW (5 MINUTES)<br>• TRAINING (50 MINUTES)<br>• END OF SESSION REVIEW (5 MINUTES) | 5<br><br>5 | • START OF SESSION REVIEW (5 MINUTES)<br>• TRAINING (50 MINUTES)<br>• END OF SESSION REVIEW (5 MINUTES) | 10 | • START OF SESSION REVIEW (5 MINUTES)<br>• TRAINING (50 MINUTES)<br>• END OF SESSION REVIEW (5 MINUTES) | 5<br><br>5 |
| 12.30–1.30 | LUNCH 60 MINUTES | | LUNCH 60 MINUTES | | LUNCH 60 MINUTES | |
| 1.30–2.30 (60 MINUTES) | • POST-LUNCH REVIEW (15 MINUTES)<br>• TRAINING (40 MINUTES)<br>• END OF SESSION REVIEW (5 MINUTES) | 15<br><br>5 | • POST-LUNCH REVIEW (15 MINUTES)<br>• TRAINING (40 MINUTES)<br>• END OF SESSION REVIEW (5 MINUTES) | 20 | • POST-LUNCH REVIEW (15 MINUTES)<br>• TRAINING (40 MINUTES)<br>• END OF SESSION REVIEW (5 MINUTES) | 15<br><br>5 |
| 2.30–2.45 | BREAK 15 MINUTES | | BREAK 15 MINUTES | | BREAK 15 MINUTES | |
| 2.45–3.45 (60 MINUTES) | • START OF SESSION REVIEW (5 MINUTES)<br>• TRAINING (50 MINUTES)<br>• END OF SESSION REVIEW (5 MINUTES) | 5<br><br>5 | • START OF SESSION REVIEW (5 MINUTES)<br>• TRAINING (50 MINUTES)<br>• END OF SESSION REVIEW (5 MINUTES) | 10 | • START OF SESSION REVIEW (5 MINUTES)<br>• TRAINING (50 MINUTES)<br>• END OF SESSION REVIEW (5 MINUTES) | 5<br><br>5 |
| 3.45–3.55 | BREAK 10 MINUTES | | BREAK 10 MINUTES | | BREAK 10 MINUTES | |
| 3.55–5.00 P.M. (65 MINUTES) | • TRAINING (25 MINUTES)<br>• END OF DAY REVIEW (30 MINUTES)<br>• SET OVERNIGHT REVIEW TASK (5 MINUTES)<br>• SUMMARY AND CLOSE (5 MINUTES) | 30<br>5 | • TRAINING (25 MINUTES)<br>• END OF DAY REVIEW (30 MINUTES)<br>• SET OVERNIGHT REVIEW TASK (5 MINUTES)<br>• SUMMARY AND CLOSE (5 MINUTES) | 35 | • END OF DAY REVIEW (45 MINUTES)<br>• SUMMARY, EVALUATION, CLOSE (15 MINUTES) | 45 |
| 5.00 P.M. | • END OF COURSE | 75 | • END OF COURSE | 105 | • END OF COURSE | 125 |
| TOT REVIEW TIME ON DAY 1 85 MINS | | | TOT REVIEW TIME ON DAY 2 115 MINS | | TOT REVIEW TIME ON DAY 3 125 MINS | |

FIGURE 7.5 // TRAINING COURSE MODEL FOR COURSES OF FOUR OR MORE DAYS

FOUR-DAY (OR MORE) TRAINING COURSE (DAYS CONSECUTIVE OR SPLIT UP) TIME OF DAY

| TIME OF DAY 8.30 A.M.– 5.00 P.M. | DAY 1 | TOTAL REVIEW TIME | DAY 2, 3, 4 (REPEAT EACH DAY) | TOTAL REVIEW TIME | LAST DAY | TOTAL REVIEW TIME |
|---|---|---|---|---|---|---|
| 8.30–10.00 (90 MINUTES) | OPENING SESSION • OPENING (20 MINUTES) • TRAINING (70 MINUTES) | 0 | OPENING SESSION • START OF DAY REVIEW (30 MINUTES) • TRAINING (50 MINUTES) | 30 | OPENING SESSION • START OF DAY REVIEW (30 MINUTES) • TRAINING (50 MINUTES) | 30 |
| 10.00–10.15 | BREAK 15 MINUTES | | BREAK 15 MINUTES | | BREAK 15 MINUTES | |
| 10.15–11.15 (60 MINUTES) | • START OF SESSION REVIEW (5 MINUTES) • TRAINING (45 MINUTES) • END OF SESSION REVIEW (5 MINUTES) | 5<br><br>5 | • START OF SESSION REVIEW (5 MINUTES) • TRAINING (45 MINUTES) • END OF SESSION REVIEW (5 MINUTES) | 5<br><br>5 | • START OF SESSION REVIEW (5 MINUTES) • TRAINING (45 MINUTES) • END OF SESSION REVIEW (5 MINUTES) | 5<br><br>5 |
| 11.15–11.30 | BREAK 15 MINUTES | | BREAK 15 MINUTES | | BREAK 15 MINUTES | |
| 11.30–12.30 (60 MINUTES) | • START OF SESSION REVIEW (5 MINUTES) • TRAINING (50 MINUTES) • END OF SESSION REVIEW (5 MINUTES) | 5<br><br>5 | • START OF SESSION REVIEW (5 MINUTES) • TRAINING (50 MINUTES) • END OF SESSION REVIEW (5 MINUTES) | 5<br><br>5 | • START OF SESSION REVIEW (5 MINUTES) • TRAINING (50 MINUTES) • END OF SESSION REVIEW (5 MINUTES) | 5<br><br>5 |
| 12.30–1.30 | LUNCH 60 MINUTES | | LUNCH 60 MINUTES | | LUNCH 60 MINUTES | |
| 1.30–2.30 (60 MINUTES) | • POST-LUNCH REVIEW (15 MINUTES) • TRAINING (40 MINUTES) • END OF SESSION REVIEW (5 MINUTES) | 15<br><br>5 | • POST-LUNCH REVIEW (15 MINUTES) • TRAINING (40 MINUTES) • END OF SESSION REVIEW (5 MINUTES) | 15<br><br>5 | • POST-LUNCH REVIEW (15 MINUTES) • TRAINING (40 MINUTES) • END OF SESSION REVIEW (5 MINUTES) | 15<br><br>5 |
| 2.30–2.45 | BREAK 15 MINUTES | | BREAK 15 MINUTES | | BREAK 15 MINUTES | |
| 2.45–3.45 (60 MINUTES) | • START OF SESSION REVIEW (5 MINUTES) • TRAINING (50 MINUTES) • END OF SESSION REVIEW • (5 MINUTES) | 5<br><br>5 | • START OF SESSION REVIEW (5 MINUTES) • TRAINING (50 MINUTES) • END OF SESSION REVIEW (5 MINUTES) | 5<br><br>5 | • START OF SESSION REVIEW (5 MINUTES) • TRAINING (50 MINUTES) • END OF SESSION REVIEW (5 MINUTES) | 5<br><br>5 |
| 3.45–3.55 | BREAK 10 MINUTES | | BREAK 10 MINUTES | | BREAK 10 MINUTES | |
| 3.55–5.00 P.M. (65 MINUTES) | • TRAINING (25 MINUTES) • END OF DAY REVIEW (30 MINUTES) • SET OVERNIGHT REVIEW TASK (5 MINUTES) • SUMMARY AND CLOSE (5 MINUTES) | 30<br><br><br>5 | • TRAINING (25 MINUTES) • END OF DAY REVIEW (30 MINUTES) • SET OVERNIGHT REVIEW TASK (5 MINUTES) • SUMMARY AND CLOSE (5 MINUTES) | 30<br><br><br>5 | • TRAINING (25 MINUTES) • END OF DAY REVIEW (30 MINUTES) | 30 |
| 5.00 | • END OF COURSE | | • END OF COURSE | | • END OF COURSE | |
| TOT REVIEW TIME ON DAY 1: 85 MINS | | | TOT REVIEW TIME ON DAY 2: 105 MINS | | TOT REVIEW TIME ON DAY 3: 110 MINS | |

# THE ROLE OF THE TRAINER DURING THE REVIEW ACTIVITY

What is the trainer's role during a review activity? When it's all over, does the trainer know that their participants know? Consider this riddle:

*When you are 'out', you are more 'in' than when you were 'in'.*

The riddle reflects how trainers conduct themselves during a review when the participants are supposed to be completing a task themselves, without trainer intervention. When you are 'out' means when you are not training and your participants are undertaking a review by themselves.

You are more 'in' means that your senses are focused and on alert, watching, listening and searching for gaps, ready to feed back all this information in the debrief and upcoming sessions.

Than when you were 'in' refers to all the logistics, content and time issues, the participant questions, the physical needs and the myriad other things a trainer is thinking about while conducting a training session.

So if you have on occasions been a 'tick in the box' trainer, then rethink your strategy. If you put more effort into conducting review activities you will certainly reap the benefits of knowing the levels of participants' knowledge, measuring their learning against your objectives and building rapport with your group because your interest in the activity further demonstrates your genuine interest in each of your participants.

# REVIEW FOR ITS OWN SAKE?

Review activities can be executed very well or very badly. This prompts the question: Should I review just for the sake of it? I refer to 'reviewing for the sake of it' as a subset of the 'tick in the box' training mentality. Consider this scenario:

A trainer arrives for the training day, plan in hand. They go through the motions of training without variation or showing genuine interest in their participants. They run the scripted review activity. During the review they sit back taking little interest in what the participants are doing during the review and how they are completing it. (In fact, they sit at the side of the training room checking their notes, then, he tidies his handouts, hangs flip charts and engages in 'busy work'.) Then, without any debrief, they do a mental 'tick off' that they have executed the review.

What purpose did the review activity serve? Who knows?

## THE TERROR OF TICK-IN-THE-BOX TRAINING

I am all too often a witness to this tick-in-the-box training style. Once these training courses are finished the trainer has scant idea whether participants have grasped the material and if they are ready to apply it to their jobs. Tick-in-the-box trainers see the review task as time to do other things, such as making themselves that much needed cup of coffee, hanging flip charts, changing the music selection or tidying tables. This mindset sees the review activity time as a time for the trainer to catch up.

Remember that to create, schedule and run the review is not enough. A solid debrief by the trainer needs to be prepared and allocated time in the training day. Without this step, you might still fall victim to tick-in-the-box training.

## HAVING GENUINE INTEREST IN YOUR PARTICIPANTS

Over the years, some participants have made a tremendous impact on me personally and professionally and others have not. But a genuine interest in participants is essential, both specifically when running review exercises and generally as a professional trainer. This does not mean delving into their personal and business lives though. Without a genuine interest in participants and what they have or have not learnt, the review activity becomes simply one more training technique.

The trainer who has a genuine interest in their participants and who genuinely wants to know how each participant is faring with the new material is actively involved in the review process. During the review have your senses on alert. Watch intently how the review is being completed. If the activity is a team review examine who is doing the work and, more important, who is not.

Listen to what is being said in discussion — what questions are being raised, what material is being referenced in manuals and workbooks? Search for the gaps. What questions are not being asked? What material is not being covered? What material is being dismissed? Feed all this information back into the debrief and then into upcoming topics.

## REVIEWING A TRAINING MYTH

Having studied the framework models provided earlier in this chapter, you might be skeptical about how you will fit all of your content PLUS the review activities into the time allowed. In Chapter 3, I explored the myth about lack of time for measuring learning. Let's review some key points about this myth.

As far as time goes, review activities are self-accommodating. When participants are feeling confident about their new skills and knowledge, they will learn at a much faster rate than if they are feeling overwhelmed and fatigued. The pace of learning is faster because of the social proof being demonstrated in the training room, the high level of confidence on the part of participants and the usefulness or relevance of the material being learnt.

As a professional trainer, my goal by the end of my training courses is for my participants to know 100%, or close to it, of all the topics that I have trained. The only way I will know this is to see evidence of it for myself, and the outcome of review activities helps me to know they know. When I am behind schedule, I would rather ensure that my participants are confident and able to apply, say, 19 out of the 20 topics than risk putting in the twentieth topic and leaving them confused and without time to recover from that confusion.

So what happens to the twentieth topic? Usually, whatever topic number it is, it is likely to take between 15 and 45 minutes to train. There are many options available to the professional trainer. Go back to Chapter 3 if you need some ideas about filling gaps in participants' knowledge.

You, the professional trainer, need to make that decision at the time of training. However, I would urge you not to risk a drop in your participants' confidence levels by cramming in more content, just so you can say you've done everything on your course outline. Your role as a professional trainer is to ensure that participants are confident enough to apply their new skills and knowledge in practice.

I rarely drop a review, preferring to drop content and measure the learning, driving home key points in preference to adding more content. I would prefer my participants to fully understand and feel confident about 80% of the material I planned to train, than have them lose much of their confidence and ability on 100%.

If I fall behind schedule, I often change my plan in some of the following ways:
- I switch some questions in the review, taking out questions that refer to the removed content.
- I execute a contingency plan, preparing a spare review that is less dependent on that last piece of content.

It certainly is tricky when you are running short of time; however, it remains the trainer's responsibility to measure and check learning in the training room.

The training experience needs to motivate participants to apply their skills and knowledge in their day-to-day lives. So review activities are scheduled strategically throughout the training day/s to refresh, invigorate and motivate learners by building their confidence. Trainers continue to be amazed by the increase in participants' learning rates when participants are engaged, motivated and confident. Review activities form a strong first step in creating this supportive learning environment.

## THE DILEMMA OF TIME AND KEEPING TO IT

Having said all this, I realise that often trainers simply run out of time. There are many reasons for this — too much discussion, activities that go over time, unrealistic allocations of time to do training tasks, or a bombardment of questions from interested participants.

When faced with this dilemma, trainers, new and seasoned alike, often look to their session plan for things to drop, and the first is often — you guessed it —the review! But, as I keep stressing, the problem with this is if you choose to drop the review for the sake of more content, you simply have to assume that your participants are confident and ready to move on.

## SUMMARY

- Professional trainers are increasingly accountable for ensuring that their course participants have learnt the material presented and are ready to apply it in the workplace.
- Reviews can't measure how successfully learnt skills will be applied, but since things not learnt can never be applied, proof of learning is an indicator of participant success.
- A review checks and measures content in a training course in a variety of different ways.
- Participants, trainers and the organisation all benefit from conducting review exercises.
- When participants are more confident and energised, trainers save training time.
- Taking a genuine interest in your participants can't be contrived — you either have a genuine interest or you do not. Analyse your motives for training on a regular basis.
- When caught short of time, drop some content from your course and review the material you have already covered.
- Build contingency plans into the review for dealing with different content if you are worried about time, or choose low-preparation reviews that do not rely heavily on covering specific content.
- During a review, the trainer should be as active as when they are training.
- During a review look for gaps in knowledge and ensure you fill these gaps during the remainder of the training course.

# CHAPTER EIGHT

# AN A–Z OF TRAINING REVIEWS

* 20 VALUABLE REVIEW IDEAS

* HOW AND WHEN TO RUN THEM

* TIPS, TRICKS AND TRAPS

LIST OF TRAINING REVIEW ACTIVITIES — ESSENTIAL DATA

| | COURSE TYPE | GROUP SIZE | TIME OF DAY | PACE | TIME TO CREATE | TIME TO RUN |
|---|---|---|---|---|---|---|
| ACRONYM ALIVE | ANY | 1–12 | ANYTIME | MODERATE | 10 MINUTES | 15 MINUTES |
| ACRONYMS DEFINED | ANY | 1–12 | ANYTIME | MODERATE | 5 MINUTES | 15 MINUTES |
| AD CAMPAIGN | ANY | UP TO 12 | POST-LUNCH, START OF DAY | SLOW AND REFLECTIVE TO MODERATE | NEGLIGIBLE | 45 MINUTES |
| BINGO SEARCH | ANY | 6–50 | ANYTIME | FAST AND COMPETITIVE | 30–40 MINUTES | 15 MINUTES |
| BINGO SHOUT | ANY | 6–50 | ANYTIME | FAST AND COMPETITIVE | 30–40 MINUTES | 15 MINUTES |
| CONCENTRATION | ANY | 4–12 | ANYTIME | MODERATE | 30 MINUTES | 20 MINUTES |
| CROSSWORD RACE | ANY | 1–12 | ANYTIME | FAST AND COMPETITIVE | 90 MINUTES | 30 MINUTES |
| DEFINITION MATCH | ANY | 1–12 | ANYTIME | MODERATE | 40 MINUTES | 20 MINUTES |
| FAST 7 — TRUTH OR LIES | ANY | 1–100 | ANYTIME | MODERATE | 10–20 MINUTES | 15 MINUTES |
| GETTING BETTER | ANY | 1–5000 | ANYTIME | SLOW AND REFLECTIVE | 10 MINUTES | 5–30 MINUTES |
| HANGMAN RULES! | ANY | 2–25 | ANYTIME | FAST AND COMPETITIVE | 40 MINUTES | 30 MINUTES |
| LEARNING LOG/ LEARNING JOURNAL | ANY | 1–5000 | ANYTIME | SLOW AND REFLECTIVE | NEGLIGIBLE | 5–20 MINUTES |
| MONEY BAGS | ANY | 4–20 | ANYTIME | FAST AND COMPETITIVE | 2 HOURS | 30 MINUTES |
| POSTCARDS OF LEARNING | ANY | 1–5000 | ANYTIME | SLOW AND REFLECTIVE | 2 HOURS* | 10 MINUTES |
| SALE OF THE MINUTE | ANY | 6-20 | END OF DAY OR END OF COURSE | FAST AND COMPETITIVE | 2–6 HOURS* | 40 MINUTES |
| SEQUENCE SHUFFLE | ANY | 4–12 | START OF SESSION, END OF SESSION OR POST-LUNCH | MODERATE | 10–30 MINUTES | 5–20 MINUTES |
| SQUAD CHALLENGE | ANY | 4–12 | ANYTIME | MODERATE | NEGLIGIBLE | 35–45 MINUTES |
| STEP MIX | ANY | 1–12 | START OF SESSION, END OF SESSION, POST-LUNCH | MODERATE | 10–30 MINUTES | 5–20 MINUTES |
| TRUE/FALSE | ANY | 1–12 | ANYTIME | MODERATE | 30 MINUTES | 15 MINUTES |
| WORDFINDER | ANY | 1–5000 | ANYTIME | MODERATE | 1–2 HOURS | 10–30 MINUTES |

*SEE INDIVIDUAL REVIEW ACTIVITY FOR FURTHER DETAILS.

| | 1. ACRONYM ALIVE | 2. ACRONYMS DEFINED | 3. AD CAMPAIGN | 4. BINGO SEARCH | 5. BINGO SHOUT | 6. CONCENTRATION | 7. CROSSWORD RACE | 8. DEFINITION MATCH | 9. FAST 7—TRUTH OR LIES | 10. GETTING BETTER | 11. HANGMAN RULES! | 12. LEARNING LOGS AND JOURNALS | 13. MONEY BAGS | 14. POSTCARDS OF LEARNING | 15. SALE OF THE MINUTE | 16. SEQUENCE SHUFFLE | 17. SQUAD CHALLENGE | 18. STEP MIX | 19. TRUE/FALSE | 20. WORDFINDER |
|---|---|---|---|---|---|---|---|---|---|---|---|---|---|---|---|---|---|---|---|---|
| ALL COURSES—ALL CONTENT TYPES | ✓ | ✓ | ✓ | ✓ | ✓ | ✓ | ✓ | ✓ | ✓ | ✓ | ✓ | ✓ | ✓ | ✓ | ✓ | ✓ | ✓ | ✓ | ✓ | ✓ |
| **SPECIFIC EXAMPLES GIVEN FOR EACH REVIEW ACTIVITY** | | | | | | | | | | | | | | | | | | | | |
| ASSERTIVENESS | | | | ✓ | | | | | | | | | | ✓ | | | | | | |
| BUSINESS WRITING | | | | | ✓ | | | | | | | | | | | | ✓ | | | |
| CAREER DEVELOPMENT | | | | | | | | | | | | | | | | | ✓ | | | |
| CHANGE MANAGEMENT | | | ✓ | | | | | | | | | | | | | | | ✓ | | |
| COMPUTER TRAINING | ✓ | ✓ | | | | ✓ | | | | | | | | | | ✓ | | | | |
| CREDIT MANAGEMENT | | | | | | | | ✓ | ✓ | | | | | | | | | | | |
| CUSTOMER SERVICE | | | | | | ✓ | | | | | ✓ | | | | | | | | | |
| INDUCTION TRAINING | ✓ | ✓ | | | | | | | | | | | | | | | | | | ✓ |
| LEADERSHIP | | | | | | | | | ✓ | | ✓ | | | | | | | | ✓ | |
| NEGOTIATION SKILLS | | | ✓ | | | | | ✓ | ✓ | | | | | | | | | | | |
| PERFORMANCE IMPROVEMENT | | | | | | | | | | | ✓ | | | | | | | ✓ | | |
| PROCESS IMPROVEMENT | | | | | | | | | | | | | | | ✓ | ✓ | | | | |
| PROJECT MANAGEMENT | | | | | | | | | | | | | ✓ | | | | | | ✓ | |
| QUALITY | | | | | | ✓ | | | | | | | | | | | | | | ✓ |
| SELLING SKILLS | | | | | | | ✓ | | | | ✓ | | | | | ✓ | | | | |
| TEAM DEVELOPMENT | | | | | | | | | | | | | | ✓ | | | | | | ✓ |
| TRAIN THE TRAINER | | | | | | | | | | | | | | ✓ | | ✓ | | | | |

# ACRONYM ALIVE

**LEARNING OUTCOMES** Challenge participants to define exactly what acronyms stand for.

**OVERVIEW** Acronyms used in the course are written on a flip chart, whiteboard or printed on a handout. One letter in each acronym is underlined, e.g. R<u>A</u>M. Participants define the underlined letter.

**IN MY EXPERIENCE...** Acronym Alive is quick to run so I like to use it as a post-lunch review or an end-of-session review.

**THE HIDDEN TWIST** The process of identifying one of the letters in the review forces participants to identify all of the letters.

**ESSENTIAL DATA**

| | |
|---|---|
| **COURSE TYPE** | Any |
| **GROUP SIZE** | 1–12 |
| **TIME OF DAY** | Any time |
| **PACE** | Moderate |
| **TIME TO CREATE** | 10 minutes |
| **TIME TO RUN** | 15 minutes (approx. 10 acronyms) |

**STEPS TO CREATE**
1. On a flip chart/whiteboard/handout list acronyms (without definitions).
2. Use a different colour or underline only one letter in each acronym.
3. Store or print until the time of the review.

**STEPS TO RUN**
1. If necessary, regroup to pairs.
2. Reveal Acronym Alive flip chart/whiteboard/give out handouts.
3. Each participant/team writes down the meaning to just the underlined/ different colour letter.

4. Check the results
    a / If using a flip chart/whiteboard: write up answers next to acronym.
    b / If using handouts: go through each acronym in turn asking the group for answers.
5. Ask debrief questions while checking the results.

## SUGGESTED DEBRIEF STRATEGY/SAMPLE QUESTIONS
- What does the A stand for in RAM?
- What do the other letters stand for in RAM?
- Where might you see this acronym?
- Who is likely to use this acronym?
- When might you use this acronym?
- Why is it important to know this acronym?
- Ask further details about the terminology, e.g. RAM: What part does RAM play in your computer?
- Ask variations of the acronym, e.g. RAM: What if I changed the A in RAM to O, as in ROM. What does this mean?

## SUGGESTED TRAINING COURSES
### COMPUTER TRAINING
From Introduction to PCs, to the most advanced desktop applications, mainframe systems or Internet training this activity will be sure to help participants learn the countless acronyms that each program includes.
### INDUCTION TRAINING
With the plethora of acronyms that are used in companies, this activity is ideal for induction training. The trainer has more evidence that participants really know what the acronyms mean.

**TIPS, TRICKS AND TRAPS** As I am conducting a training course, I keep listening for participants' use of acronyms. When I hear an acronym used, I always ask what it stands for. I am often amazed how many acronyms are part of day-to-day corporate language and how often I don't know what it means! In your courses ensure that participant know the acronym plus its meaning.

# ACRONYMS DEFINED

 **LEARNING OUTCOMES** To ensure that when participants speak in acronyms they know what they mean

 **OVERVIEW** Run throughout the entire course, this review constantly reminds participants of the definition of acronyms used within the training course. A flip chart headed 'Acronyms Defined' is created and hung on the wall. At the end of each session, before a break, the trainer and participants update the flip chart with acronyms and their meanings that were discovered during that session.

  **IN MY EXPERIENCE...** This is a great review for technical training where acronyms are often used. Also, this review is fabulous for induction training.

 **THE HIDDEN TWIST** This is a great training ritual. Participants get to know that before each break, they go to the acronym flip chart. It helps reinforce all acronyms used, not just the new one/s that session.

 **ESSENTIAL DATA**

| | |
|---|---|
| **COURSE TYPE** | Any |
| **GROUP SIZE** | 1–12 |
| **TIME OF DAY** | Any time |
| **PACE** | Moderate |
| **TIME TO CREATE** | 5 minutes |
| **TIME TO RUN** | 15 minutes, 1 minute each time an acronym is added |

 **STEPS TO CREATE**
1. Create a flip chart with the heading 'Acronyms Defined'
2. Store until the training begins.

**STEPS TO RUN**
1. After each session, just before the break, have participants put the newly learnt acronym and its definition on the flip chart.
2. Build the flip chart throughout the entire duration of the course.

### SUGGESTED DEBRIEF STRATEGY/SAMPLE QUESTIONS

- Where might you see this acronym?
- What does the acronym stand for?
- Where did you first hear this acronym used?
- Why is this acronym used?
- Who is likely to use this acronym?
- When might you use this acronym?
- Why is it important to know this acronym?
- What other terms that we've covered today relate to this acronym?
  Ask further details about the terminology, e.g. RAM: What part does RAM play in your computer?
- Ask variations of the acronym, e.g. RAM: What if I changed the A in RAM to O, as in ROM. What does this mean?

### WORKING EXAMPLE

#### COMPUTER TRAINING

Collect the commonly used acronyms from the topic.

#### INDUCTION TRAINING

Collect the commonly used acronyms from the organisation. This may include division names, product lines, supplier codes and so on.

**TIPS, TRICKS AND TRAPS** At the end of the course, remove the flip chart, then have participants compete in groups to recall as many acronyms as possible, along with their definitions.

# AD CAMPAIGN

 **LEARNING OUTCOMES** Participants sell their key learning point to the rest of the group in the form of an newspaper advertisement.

 **OVERVIEW** Participants review the entire course and make a list of their key learnings. From this list they choose their #1 key learning. Each participant is given a large sheet of paper on which to draw an advertisement for a magazine or newspaper selling their #1 key learning.

 **IN MY EXPERIENCE...** This is a fabulous review to get participants to add depth to their key learnings. The advertisements then make a great display in the training room.

 **THE HIDDEN TWIST** In order for participants to sell their key learning to the rest of the group they must have a deep understanding of the content. The articulation of key learnings helps auditory learners, drawing the ad helps visual learners and the presentation of it to the rest of the group helps kinesthetic learners. As a trainer you can see where participants are focused. Also look for gaps. If no one has a #1 key learning on the key goal of the course (from your perspective) then you need to rectify the situation!

 **ESSENTIAL DATA**

| | |
|---|---|
| **COURSE TYPE** | Any |
| **GROUP SIZE** | Up to 12 |
| **TIME OF DAY** | Post-lunch or start-of-day (for multi-day courses) activity |
| **PACE** | Slow and reflective, then moderate |
| **TIME TO CREATE** | Negligible |
| **TIME TO RUN** | 45 minutes |

 **STEPS TO CREATE**
1. Ensure you have large sheets of paper and coloured markers (of various styles) available for participants to use.

 **STEPS TO RUN**
1. Participants list their own key learnings from the entire course (allow no more than five minutes.

2. Participants choose their #1 key learning.
3. Participants design an advertisement to sell their #1 key learning to the rest of the group (allow 15 minutes). The advertisement should include:
   • A slogan; a picture or symbol
   • It would be likely to appear in a colour magazine.
4. Each participant presents their advertisement to the rest of the group. This should be a sales pitch to accompany the advertisement.
5. Post advertisements on the training room wall.

## SUGGESTED DEBRIEF STRATEGY/SAMPLE QUESTIONS
• Discuss common themes in advertisements.
• The trainer should ask 'why' and 'what if' questions to add depth to the learning.

## WORKING EXAMPLE
### NEGOTIATION SKILLS
In negotiation skills, we use this review to begin the second day of the two-day training course. On the evening of day 1, an overnight review is set where participants are asked to create their list of key learnings (see review activity: Hot Tips). Using this list, participants choose their #1 Hot Tip, then create their advertisement.

### CHANGE MANAGEMENT
In a one-day training course on change this review activity can be used after lunch. To have this activity run smoothly, have participants choose their key learning points before lunch. As a post-lunch review, have participants choose their #1 learning point and create an advertisement to present to the whole group.

## TIPS, TRICKS AND TRAPS
• If participants tell you they are artistically challenged encourage them to create a symbol or icon for their advertisement.
• If participants have difficulty starting off the drawing of their advertisement, encourage them to simply start with a border on the page. Once they have 'marked' the page, they seem encouraged to continue with the rest of the advertisement.
• Award prizes for originality, creativity, innovation, artistic licence and so on.

# BINGO SEARCH

**LEARNING OUTCOMES** To have participants answer 12 questions about the training topic.

**OVERVIEW** Each participant is given a handout with 12 questions on it. Participants must interview others in the group to find the answers. The participant who can get answers to all questions first shouts 'bingo' and is awarded a prize.

**IN MY EXPERIENCE...** If you like noisy, fast-paced training activities then this review is for you!

**THE HIDDEN TWIST** The participants are so engrossed in the competition they don't notice that really what they are doing is a test of 12 questions!

**ESSENTIAL DATA**

| | |
|---|---|
| **COURSE TYPE** | Any |
| **GROUP SIZE** | 6–50 |
| **TIME OF DAY** | Any time |
| **PACE** | Fast and competitive |
| **TIME TO CREATE** | 30–40 minutes |
| **TIME TO RUN** | 15 minutes |

**STEPS TO CREATE**

1. Create 12 questions that will generate reasonably short answers.
2. Using three columns and four rows, create a handout to resemble a bingo sheet. Each box will contain a question.
3. Print one per participant.

**STEPS TO RUN**

1. Give each participant a handout.
2. Explain the activity rules:
   - The aim is to be the first finished with answers to each of the 12 questions.
   - You must interview 12 different people (or, for smaller groups, everyone, at least once).

- Ask the person the question, write the answer on your handout.
- When you have all 12 answers shout 'bingo'.
3. When a participant shouts 'bingo', stop the activity and have them read their answers to the whole group.
4. If all answers are correct award the prize to the winning participant.
5. If there is an incorrect answer: continue playing until someone else shouts 'bingo', check again, then award the prize.

### SUGGESTED DEBRIEF STRATEGY/SAMPLE QUESTIONS
- Discuss each of the 12 questions and the answers for each.
- The trainer should ask 'why' and 'what if' questions to add depth to the learning.

### WORKING EXAMPLE
**ASSERTIVENESS**
See page 137.

**TIPS, TRICKS AND TRAPS** Modify the number of questions to equal the number of participants. Ensure that there is still a minimum of six questions and no more than 15 questions, otherwise the activity may take too long.

# BINGO SHOUT

**LEARNING OUTCOMES** A team-based competition to review course terms and definitions.

**OVERVIEW** Bingo Shout is a high-concentration, fast-paced review that ensures active involvement and high energy from every participant in the group. Each team is given a handout with answers on it. The first team to mark off five in a row shouts 'bingo'.

**IN MY EXPERIENCE...** This is a fantastic end-of-day review or end-of-course review. It creates a great team atmosphere while reviewing the key terms and definitions from the training.

**THE HIDDEN TWIST** The participants are so engrossed in the competition they don't notice that really what they are doing is a test of up to 35, questions and building teamwork at the same time.

**ESSENTIAL DATA**

| | |
|---|---|
| **COURSE TYPE** | Any |
| **GROUP SIZE** | 6–50 |
| **TIME OF DAY** | Any time |
| **PACE** | Fast and competitive |
| **TIME TO CREATE** | 30–40 minutes |
| **TIME TO RUN** | 15 minutes |

**STEPS TO CREATE**

1. Choose 35 course terms that have short definitions (25 will have corresponding answers, 10 won't — however, it still 'tests' the participants). Write a 'trainers guide' with each question and answer listed.
2. Using three columns and four rows, create a handout to resemble a bingo sheet. Each box will contain a answer.
3. Print one handout per team (approximately 3–5 participants per team). (I enlarge this on a photocopier to fit on the largest sheet possible.)
4. Plan the order of questions so that teams are asked as many of the 35 questions as possible in order to shout 'bingo'.

## STEPS TO RUN

1. Give each team a handout.
2. Explain the activity rules:
   - As I ask a question or say a term look for the answer on your answer sheet.
   - When you find the correct answer cross it through.
   - When your team gets five answers in a row, shout 'bingo'.
3. Read each of the questions (allowing approximately five seconds for teams to find their answers).
4. Check the results of the winning team. If correct, award prizes, otherwise continue playing until another team shouts 'bingo', check again, then award the prizes.

## SUGGESTED DEBRIEF STRATEGY/SAMPLE QUESTIONS

- Discuss a random number of the questions (where participants had the most difficulty) and the answers for each.
- The trainer should ask 'why' and 'what if' questions to add depth to the learning.

## WORKING EXAMPLE

**BUSINESS WRITING**

See page 138.

**TIPS, TRICKS AND TRAPS** In small groups this review activity can also be run in pairs or individually. So that all participants don't shout 'bingo' at once, reorder the answer sheets so that you have several versions as handouts. This review sounds deceptively simple; however, you may be surprised at how competitive adults will become when they are competing for a prize.

# CONCENTRATION (MEMORY GAME)

**LEARNING OUTCOMES** Based on the childhood game, Concentration is a small-group activity that has participants match training terms with their definitions.

**OVERVIEW** Twenty cards in two colours are laid face down on the table. One colour is for terms, the other for definitions. Teams take turns turning over one term and definition card looking for a match. The team with the most matches wins.

**IN MY EXPERIENCE...** I use this as a post-lunch review activity to review terms and definitions that have been presented in the morning session. This is an activity of true team involvement that has all teams equally involved during the whole game.

**THE HIDDEN TWIST** Teams are focused on remembering where cards are placed and whether the term matches the definition. Because of this concentration element, they forget they are doing a test of 10 terms and definitions!

**ESSENTIAL DATA**

| | |
|---|---|
| **COURSE TYPE** | Any |
| **GROUP SIZE** | 4–12 |
| **TIME OF DAY** | Any time. Particularly good as post-lunch review. |
| **PACE** | Moderate |
| **TIME TO CREATE** | 30 minute |
| **TIME TO RUN** | 20 minutes |

**STEPS TO CREATE**

1. Collect 10 key terms that have been covered in the training course. Write definitions to the terms.
2. Create small cards (approximately the size of playing cards) in two colours.
3. Choose a colour for terms; write terms.
4. Use the other colour for definitions.
5. Create an answer sheet for the trainer.
6. Collect prizes for winners and other players.

**STEPS TO RUN**

1. Mix up cards and lay out face-down. See page 139.

2. Regroup participants into small groups (3–5 participants) (works best if no more than three teams).
3. Have participants move around the table on which cards are laid.
4. Explain the rules:
   - The aim of the activity is to collect matched cards. The team with the most cards at the end wins.
   - Each team takes turns turning over a term card and a definition card. Do not remove the cards from their spot; simply flip them over.
   - Read what appears on the cards out loud as it is revealed.
   - If the team determines that the term matches the definition then give them permission to remove both cards from the table, if not turn both cards face down again.
   - You will have to concentrate and use the whole team to remember where the matched cards are.
5. Run the review activity. Ensure that teams read the statements aloud, as this reinforces learning.
6. Award prizes for the winning team and consolation prizes for all other players.

## SUGGESTED DEBRIEF STRATEGY/SAMPLE QUESTIONS
- During the review activity, the trainer should be aware of statements that are causing the most difficulty.
- After the review activity is over the trainer should ask 'why' and 'what if' questions to add depth to the learning and to ensure that 'sticking points' are overcome.

## WORKING EXAMPLE
### QUALITY
Cards with generic terms of quality, policy, core values, 'walking the talk', customer needs, contribution, limitation, teamwork, cooperation, competition, vendors can be included. More specific terms such as flow chart, histograms, pareto chart, work breakdown structure, process, total cost, continuous improvement and variation might also be used.

**TIPS, TRICKS AND TRAPS** Create no more than 20 cards. This is a deceptively difficult activity and more than 20 cards will prove frustrating and overly time consuming.

# CROSSWORD RACE

**LEARNING OUTCOMES** Teams race to complete crosswords.

**OVERVIEW** This review is simply a disguised test of 40 questions.

**IN MY EXPERIENCE...** From junior staff to senior leaders this activity gets participants moving and working faster than before. I allow participants to use whatever resource material they have on hand to complete the crossword. If both teams stall, I might give them a single letter to kickstart the race again.

**THE HIDDEN TWIST** Teams are so intensely focused on the competitive nature of the review activity that they forget that they are really just answering examination questions!

## ESSENTIAL DATA

| | |
|---|---|
| **COURSE TYPE** | Any |
| **GROUP SIZE** | 6–12 |
| **TIME OF DAY** | Any time. Particularly good as start-of-session, end-of-session, or post-lunch activity. |
| **PACE** | Fast and competitive |
| **TIME TO CREATE** | 90 minutes (using a computerised crossword maker) |
| **TIME TO RUN** | 30 minutes |

## STEPS TO CREATE

1. Purchase a crossword maker, and key in statements and clues.
2. Print a blank crossword and enlarge it to poster size.
3. Print question sheets (clue sheets) for each participant.
4. Print an answer sheet for the trainer. (Spare copies of the completed puzzle can be given to participants as a handout.)
5. Have prizes on hand for winning team (mini-chocolate bars or similar).

## STEPS TO RUN

1. Hang blank crossword puzzles on opposite sides of the training room walls.
2. Regroup participants into small groups (3–5). Up to four teams works well.
3. Assign each group a puzzle.
4. Explain the rules:

- You need to work as a team to complete the crossword.
- You can use any resource materials you like to help you.
- When your team has finished, shout 'finished'.

5. Give each participant a clue sheet and then shout 'go!'
6. When a team shouts 'finished', stop the race.
7. With the whole group, have the finished team tell you all the answers.
   - If all answers are correct, then award winning prizes
   - If an answer is incorrect, restart the race until a winner is declared.

## SUGGESTED DEBRIEF STRATEGY/SAMPLE QUESTIONS
- The trainer should be aware of questions that are causing difficulty.
- After the race has finished the trainer should ask 'why' and 'what if' questions to add depth to the learning and to ensure that 'sticking points' are overcome.

## WORKING EXAMPLE
### SELLING SKILLS
Usually the outgoing nature of sales people accords well with this high-energy test of skill. Questions and statements can be focused on attitude, planning, behaviour, product knowledge, prospecting and getting appointments, customer needs, appearance, preparation, sales call openings, building rapport, communication skills, questioning, presenting solutions, presentation skills, handling objections, difficult situations, gaining commitment, closing the sale, record keeping and follow up.

## TIPS, TRICKS AND TRAPS
- Make the questions specific. That is, there should be a definitive answer.
- Make the clues short. Clues should be no more than 10 words. Clues should be presented as follows: 'Put a _____ line where the answer fits. (5)'
- The clue sheet should fit onto no more than one page.
- Make the answers only one word. Answers should include the number of letters.
- Keep the groups moving. There may be some difficulties, so ensure that you are actively involved in checking participants' progress throughout the entire review activity.
- Give hints as necessary. Often a letter can help keep a group from stalling. I simply walk up to their crossword and without saying anything write in a single letter. Remember that you are there to help participants to learn!

# DEFINITION MATCH

**LEARNING OUTCOMES** To ensure that participants know the definitions of important terms used throughout the course.

**OVERVIEW** A whole-group activity where participants match cards with terms and definitions. Each participant is given at least one card to ensure that everyone is involved.

**IN MY EXPERIENCE...** Some terms in training courses have very similar, yet importantly different, definitions. This is a way to ensure that participants know the correct definitions.

**THE HIDDEN TWIST** The last couple of card matches are usually a process of elimination. I often include a blank card on which participants must write the last definition themselves. Alternatively, an extra definition or two incorrect definitions may be added to the card sort. This way, participants must overcome the trap thereby adding depth to their learning.

**ESSENTIAL DATA**

| | |
|---|---|
| **COURSE TYPE** | Any |
| **GROUP SIZE** | 1–12 |
| **TIME OF DAY** | Any time. Particularly good as end-of-session, start-of-session, post-lunch and as an end-of-day review activity. |
| **PACE** | Moderate |
| **TIME TO CREATE** | 40 minutes |
| **TIME TO RUN** | 20 minutes (approx. 10 terms and 10 definitions) |

**STEPS TO CREATE**

1. Choose 10 key terms and write definitions for them.
2. Create cards in two colours.
3. Choose a colour for terms; write or print the terms.
4. Use the other colour to write or print the definitions.
5. Create an answer sheet for the trainer.
6. Create a card that says 'term' and another that says 'definition'.
7. Put tape or Blu Tac on the backs of all remaining cards and place face down until you are ready to run the activity.

## STEPS TO RUN
1. High up on a training room wall place the cards stating 'term' and 'definition'.
2. Have participants stand up near these cards.
3. Hand out the cards randomly until all are distributed. (It doesn't matter if one participant has more than another.)
4. Have participants put terms and definitions in order beneath the 'term' and 'definition' cards.
5. Once completed, the trainer reads each term with its associated definition. If it is correct, then further questioning and discussion can take place to add depth to the learning.

## SUGGESTED DEBRIEF STRATEGY/SAMPLE QUESTIONS
- Where might you see this term?
- Who is likely to use this term?
- When might you use this term?
- Why is it important to know this definition?
- Ask further 'why' and 'what if' type questions to add depth to the learning.

## SUGGESTED TRAINING COURSES
### COMPUTER TRAINING
Choose the terms that participants must know from the training and write definitions accordingly.
### CUSTOMER SERVICE
Common customer service terms such as competition, customer needs, quality, active listening, initiative, customer value, delight, service cycle, moments of truth and customer feedback are some that might be used in a definition match for customer service.

**TIPS, TRICKS AND TRAPS** Use the glossaries found in reference manuals, participant workbooks, books and other course development aids to help you quickly create this review activity.

# FAST 7 — TRUTH OR LIES

**LEARNING OUTCOMES** An individual review activity of seven statements that are either true or false.

**OVERVIEW** This is a review activity that can be slotted into a training course for use almost anywhere during the day.

**IN MY EXPERIENCE...** I include this review activity in participant workbooks at the end of a section or topic. I have also created statements on cards and as a handout.

**THE HIDDEN TWIST** This is such a quick review activity the participants do it without even realising they are doing a review! It is so fast that they have done it before they know it.

**ESSENTIAL DATA**

| | |
|---|---|
| **COURSE TYPE** | Any |
| **GROUP SIZE** | 1–100 |
| **TIME OF DAY** | Any time. Particularly good as start-of-session, end-of-session, post-lunch or overnight task. |
| **PACE** | Moderate |
| **TIME TO CREATE** | 10–20 minutes |
| **TIME TO RUN** | 15 minutes |

**STEPS TO CREATE**

1. Write seven true or false statements.
2. Include them within a participant workbook, create a flip chart, handouts or print onto cards (as a team sort).

**STEPS TO RUN**

1. Have participants answer true or false to each statement.
2. When all participants have finished go through each statement.
3. If the answer is true, ask 'why' and 'what if' questions to add depth to the learning.
4. If the answer is false, ask 'what would make this true?'

## SUGGESTED DEBRIEF STRATEGY/SAMPLE QUESTIONS

• The trainer should ask 'why' and 'what if' questions to add depth to the learning.
  'What would make this true?'
  'What other topics are related here?'
  'Why is this important?'
  'What makes this statement different from _____?'
  'How can you apply this when you return to your job?'
  [for a false statement] 'What would happen if you did this?'

## WORKING EXAMPLE

### CREDIT MANAGEMENT

For each of the following statements write T (True) or F (False) in the right column.

|  | |
|---|---|
| 1. CREDIT IS ONLY A FINANCIAL ISSUE FOR CREDIT STAFF | |
| 2. WE GIVE CREDIT TO HELP THE ON-GOING RELATIONSHIP WITH OUR CUSTOMERS | |
| 3. DSO STANDS FOR DAYS SALES OUTSTANDING | |
| 4. THINGS THAT ARE IMPORTANT TO CUSTOMERS INCLUDE INTEREST FREE FINANCE AND US GETTING THEIR INVOICES CORRECT THE FIRST TIME | |
| 5. GIVING CREDIT HELPS US COMPETE | |
| 6. TRADING TERMS ARE 45 DAYS FROM THE DATE OF SALE | |
| 7. THE CREDIT DEPARTMENT WILL ONLY HELP ACCOUNT MANAGERS WHEN OPENING ACCOUNTS AND CHASING BAD DEBTS | |

### NEGOTIATION SKILLS

Where there is controversy, be sure to listen to the reasoning of both sides. Listen to participants who think it is true and to those who think a statement is false. Hearing both sides of the discussion has positive effects for all participants.

**TIPS, TRICKS AND TRAPS** Remember, there is no learning for participants in 'false'. When we say 'Don't think of a giraffe' you can't help but think of a giraffe! We must embed the true answer in the participant's mind, not the false one. Always ask 'what would make this statement true' to ensure that participants know the correct answer.

# GETTING BETTER

**LEARNING OUTCOMES** An individual review activity that asks action-based questions that encourage reflection on skills.

**OVERVIEW** The trainer prepares two or three questions as a handout, on a flip chart or in the participant workbook. Individually participants answer the questions and share their answers in small teams or with the whole group.

**IN MY EXPERIENCE...** Adult education would take a huge leap forward if every trainer simply stopped for five minutes every hour and asked two or three reflective questions that prompted participants to say how they will improve the effectiveness and application of their learning.

**THE HIDDEN TWIST** This review ensures that participants make the connection from the training room to their real-life environment. Invoking the social influence pattern of commitment and consistency means participants are more likely to do what they say they will do.

**ESSENTIAL DATA**

| | |
|---|---|
| **COURSE TYPE** | Any |
| **GROUP SIZE** | 1–5000 |
| **TIME OF DAY** | Any time. Particularly good as start- or end-of-session activity. |
| **PACE** | Slow and reflective |
| **TIME TO CREATE** | 10 minutes |
| **TIME TO RUN** | 5–30 minutes |

**STEPS TO CREATE**

1. Create two or three 'thinking questions' that will challenge participants to reflect on their current skill level and then plan for improvement.
2. Add these to a participant workbook, write on a flip chart or whiteboard.

**STEPS TO RUN**

1. Ensure that the learning environment is quiet and free from distraction.
2. Ask the question and ensure that participants work individually on their answers. Try to keep participants quiet even if some are finished.
3. Whole-group debrief; ask for responses randomly.

4. Or small-group debrief: regroup to small groups (3–5 participants). Have them discuss each others' answers and then share with whole group.

   **OPTION:** Create a Group Action Plan flip chart.

   Have participants from each group create an Our Actions flip chart and present to the whole group. This way they are even more likely to be committed to their planned actions.

## SUGGESTED DEBRIEF STRATEGY/SAMPLE QUESTIONS

- After hearing their planned actions, the trainer can engage in a whole-group discussion about barriers, blocks and implications and a success strategy for implementing the plan.
- Questions such as:

   What barriers might get in your way?

   Who else needs to be involved?

   Is there anyone you should talk to before doing this?

   What are the implications of these actions?

   What are the benefits of this plan?

   How will you know when you are successful?

## WORKING EXAMPLE

### CREDIT MANAGEMENT

Which areas of being proactive with credit would you like to improve?

How will you achieve these improvements?

### LEADERSHIP SKILLS

What actions will you take in setting a vision and clear goals for your team?

How will you support others' good ideas and help get them implemented?

How can you create an open-door policy and be more accessible for those who report to you?

### NEGOTIATION SKILLS

The single most useful weapon in negotiation is preparation. What can you do differently from now on to be better prepared?

## TIPS, TRICKS AND TRAPS

Ensure that you remain quiet during the activity. Sitting at the side of the room quietly is better than being at the front rustling paper and causing a distraction.

# HANGMAN RULES!

 **LEARNING OUTCOMES** Based on the reverse of the childhood game hangman, participants need to answer 12 questions faster than the opposing teams to create their hangman and win a prize.

 **OVERVIEW** A whole-group activity that has participants in up to four teams. Using a beat the buzzer format, participants race to answer the question correctly first to be awarded a part of their hangman.

 **IN MY EXPERIENCE...** As teams get closer and closer to the finished hangman, competition fires up and team work is intense. If you like fast action-based review activities, then this one is for you.

 **THE HIDDEN TWIST** This review activity is one of listening and knowledge. It is simply a disguise for a test of 40 questions.

 **ESSENTIAL DATA**

| | |
|---|---|
| **COURSE TYPE** | Any |
| **GROUP SIZE** | 2–25 |
| **TIME OF DAY** | Any time. Particularly good as post-lunch or end-of-day review. |
| **PACE** | Fast and competitive |
| **TIME TO CREATE** | 40 minutes (based on 15 questions) |
| **TIME TO RUN** | 30 minutes |

 **STEPS TO CREATE**

1. Write 15 questions. (12 + 3 spare). The answers should be short, like true or false or terms or definitions.
2. Prepare a flip chart or whiteboard with the heading 'Hangman Rules' on it. A sample 12-stroke hangman can be put in the corner.
3. Collect prizes for the winning team and all other players.
4. Have a noisemaking device for each team (bells, maracas, mini-drums, etc.).

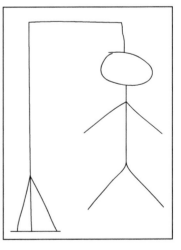

### STEPS TO RUN

1. Regroup to small teams (3–5 participants).
2. Explain rules:
   - The aim is to answer questions faster than your opposing team and create your hangman first.
   - All questions will be asked for all teams to answer.
   - The first team to buzz in will have a chance to answer.
   - Each correct answer will give you another part of your hangman. There are 12 parts to our hangman.
   - An incorrect answer will give other teams a further chance to buzz in with an answer.
3. Ask each question.
4. When a team wins, award prizes.

### SUGGESTED DEBRIEF STRATEGY/SAMPLE QUESTIONS

At the end of the review activity, if there was difficulty or dispute about some questions ensure that you clarify the answer before moving on with further training content.

### SUGGESTED TRAINING COURSES

#### PERFORMANCE IMPROVEMENT

Hangman questions might include questions about change, performance review forms, timing of performance reviews, giving feedback, managing difficult situations, setting goals and the work environment.

#### CUSTOMER SERVICE

Hangman questions might include questions about customer needs, competition, the process of customer feedback, collating customer service data, customer behaviour types, meetings with customers and handling customer complaints.

**TIPS, TRICKS AND TRAPS** As a trainer you need to concentrate on which team is 'buzzing' first. Often a co-trainer can be the 'buzz' monitor. Alternatively, devices with buzzers and lights are available for games use.

# LEARNING LOGS/JOURNALS

**LEARNING OUTCOMES** To have participants reflect on their learning and how they will apply their new knowledge and/or skills.

**OVERVIEW** Participants are given a learning log or learning journal that they regularly update throughout the course. Time is given to participants for quiet reflective analysis of their key learnings and how they will apply them.

**IN MY EXPERIENCE...** In music, phrasing adds the essential breathing space to all compositions, whether fast or slow. Likewise in training, continuous review activities add intervals for participants to stop and consolidate their learning. Creating a learning journal is beneficial for learners who prefer individual, intrapersonal and reflective activities. All participants benefit from transferring the learnt theory into practical applications.

**THE HIDDEN TWIST** This reflective time allows participants to recharge their batteries and get ready for the new information in the next session. Also, participants listen to how others will apply their knowledge. When participants share how they will use their knowledge it helps to keep negative participants at bay. Because their peers are positive and willing to apply the material they will be less likely to remain negative.

**ESSENTIAL DATA**

| | |
|---|---|
| **COURSE TYPE** | Any |
| **GROUP SIZE** | 1–5000 |
| **TIME OF DAY** | Any time. Particularly good as end-of-session or start-of-session or overnight review. |
| **PACE** | Slow and reflective |
| **TIME TO CREATE** | Negligible |
| **TIME TO RUN** | 5–20 minutes |

**STEPS TO CREATE**

1. Create a section in the participant guide with the following headings:
   - Key learnings
   - How I will apply my key learnings.
2. Call this Learning Log or Learning Journal.

## STEPS TO RUN

1. At various times of the day give participants some quiet time to consolidate their learning in their learning log or learning journal.
2. Have participants update their learning log or learning journal regularly throughout the course. (Either before or after a break, or at the end of each major section of the training course.)

OPTIONAL: At the end of the course, have participants consolidate their learning log or learning journal into an action plan with timelines and measurable results.

## SUGGESTED DEBRIEF STRATEGY/SAMPLE QUESTIONS

Throughout the course as each learning journal updating session is completed have participants tell the whole group their #1 key learning.

## SUGGESTED TRAINING COURSES

### SALES

In a fast-paced sales training course, creating a learning journal is an ideal way to build in individual reflective time that helps to consolidate learnings and begin the transfer of learning to the workplace. When seeking ideas on how to apply learnings, participants could devise an individual customer action plan.

### LEADERSHIP

A learning journal is a key tool to assist with the transfer of leadership concepts and models into practical application. Participants who create learning journal entries throughout the training course will more likely find it easier to consolidate an action plan and then apply the actions in their day-to-day work.

## TIPS, TRICKS AND TRAPS

- In a two-day training course I usually stop six or seven times to allow participants to update their learning journal. Either before or after each break I allow 5 to 10 minutes of quiet reflective time. Put on some quiet classical music to enhance the tranquil setting.
- By the end of a two-day training course, participants have usually completed about six pages of key learnings together with application ideas. As one of the final activities, their learning journal is then consolidated into an action plan. This action plan is shared with their manager on their return to their workplace and a plan for its implementation is formulated.

# MONEY BAGS (JEOPARDY)

**LEARNING OUTCOMES** To ensure participants know the key learning points to the training course and to re-energise the group in a fun and competitive way.

**OVERVIEW** This is a fast-paced training review that is often used as 'Jeopardy'. In teams, participants 'beat the buzzer' to answer 12 questions correctly. A board of 12 money bags is divided into three categories. Behind each bag is a question; the higher the dollar value, the more difficult the question.

**IN MY EXPERIENCE...** Even if participants have played Money bags before, I never cease to marvel at their competitive drive to win! This is a great review activity at the end of a course to re-energise even the most jaded and tired learner!

**THE HIDDEN TWIST** Money bags is simply a test of 12 questions; however, participants are so involved in the game that they don't notice.

**ESSENTIAL DATA**

| | |
|---|---|
| **COURSE TYPE** | Any |
| **GROUP SIZE** | 4–20 |
| **TIME OF DAY** | Any time. Particularly good as an end-of-day or end-of-course review. |
| **PACE** | Fast and competitive |
| **TIME TO CREATE** | 2 hours |
| **TIME TO RUN** | 30 minutes |

**STEPS TO CREATE**

1. Using a piece of heavy poster board or a piece of flip chart paper create a Money bags board.
   - Put the heading Money bags at the top.
   - Create three categories of questions (e.g. major sections of the course or generic categories like 'quick ways', 'fast cash', 'tips and tricks', etc.).
   - Cut out 12 money bags.
   - Create three sets of $100, $250, $350 and $500 bags.
   - Using velcro dots or Blu Tac, stick the money bags to the board.
2. Write four questions for each of the three categories. They should range in degree of difficulty. The higher the dollar value of the bag the more difficult the question.
3. Collect noisemakers and prizes for each team.

## STEPS TO RUN

1. Regroup participants into small groups (3–5 participants).
2. Have each group think of a team name. Display this name on their table.
3. Give each team a noisemaker.
4. Explain the rules of the game:
   - The aim of Money bags is to collect as much money as possible.
   - Each money bag has a question associated with it.
   - This is a beat-the-buzzer game. Your team needs to buzz in first in order to get a chance to answer.
   - A correct answer wins the money. An incorrect answer allows other groups to 'buzz in'.
5. Have teams test their buzzers.
6. As a team answers correctly, give them the money bag (this saves you from keeping score) and award prizes and consolation prizes accordingly.

## SUGGESTED DEBRIEF STRATEGY/SAMPLE QUESTIONS

Take notice of any areas of learning in which participants are having difficulty and ensure that any gaps in their learning are filled before continuing with more content.

## WORKING EXAMPLE

### PROJECT MANAGEMENT

On a multi-day project management course, play Money bags at the end of each day and carry the scores forward. Category names might include: 'PM Tools', 'Charts & Smarts' (questions on graphs and charts, and smart ways of working), 'Work Time' (questions about timelines, planning, work breakdowns, etc.) or 'When things go wrong!' (questions on contingency planning etc.).

### CAREER DEVELOPMENT

As a great energiser at the end of a training course on career development, choose categories such as 'Where I am now', 'Options Galore' and 'Smart Moves'.

## TIPS, TRICKS AND TRAPS

I have a generic Money bags board in my collection of review activities. The only thing that changes on the Money bags board is the category names (which I put on each time using Post-it notes). I create the questions on a single sheet of paper and store it with the trainer's guide.

# POSTCARDS OF LEARNING

 **LEARNING OUTCOMES** To have participants reflect on their learning and how they will apply their new knowledge and/or skills.

 **OVERVIEW** This is a continuing activity that has participants write a postcard about their key learning from each major section of the training course. They then 'post' the postcard to themselves. They receive their postcards after the the training as a reminder of their learnings and a kick-start to their action plan.

 **IN MY EXPERIENCE...** This activity is a continuing review activity that is run over the entire duration of a training course. It is important to give participants 5 to 10 minutes of quiet time at least three times a day to complete postcards.

 **THE HIDDEN TWIST** This is a totally individual activity. This way, the personalisation and confidentiality of what is written is maintained. It is usually a great surprise for participants to receive their postcards a couple of weeks after the course when they read (and therefore review) what they learnt.

 **ESSENTIAL DATA**

| | |
|---|---|
| **COURSE TYPE** | Any |
| **GROUP SIZE** | 1–5000 |
| **TIME OF DAY** | Any time. Particularly good as end-of-session or start-of-session activity. |
| **PACE** | Slow and reflective |
| **TIME TO CREATE** | 2 hours (depending on how many and how elaborate the postcards are) |
| **TIME TO RUN** | 10 minutes for each postcard |

 **STEPS TO CREATE**
1. Create standard-format postcards for each major section of learning.
2. On the front put the topic name and an identifying graphic.
3. Create a mailbox. A cardboard box covered in red paper will suffice.

 **STEPS TO RUN**
1. At the end of each major section give participants time to write a postcard to themselves to consolidate their learning.
2. Give suggestions on what to write:

- Key learning point.
- How this topic might be actioned.
- Things that might get in your way and how to overcome them.
- Other things to be remembered from this section.

3. Remind them that this time should be quiet time.
4. Encourage participants to use a variety of styles (written, symbols, etc.)
5. Have them address the postcard to themselves and post it in the mailbox.
6. After the course has finished, sort the postcards by participant, put into a sealed envelope and post two weeks after the completion of the course. Include a sustaining activity or a reminder about the next stage of learning.

## SUGGESTED DEBRIEF STRATEGY/SAMPLE QUESTIONS
Ensure that any gaps in learning are filled before proceeding with the next topic.

## SUGGESTED TRAINING COURSES
### TRAIN THE TRAINER
In the busy lives of trainers we are often the 'plumber with the leaky pipes'! When participants receive their postcards a couple of weeks later they will review key points and kick-start their action plans.
### ASSERTIVENESS
When training courses involve participants undergoing behavioural shifts, sustaining activities assist in keeping the concepts alive until the new behaviour becomes integrated. Postcards of learning will remind participants of the difference between passive, assertive and aggressive behaviours and help enforce spoken language phraseology and body language signals.

**TIPS, TRICKS AND TRAPS** This is one of the simplest and most successful metacognitive and reflective review activities that I run. A trap to avoid is not to shortchange participants with time for writing their postcards. Some participants will naturally complete this activity quicker than others. To assist with this, I have a crossword (based on the content of the course) that I give faster participants to do while waiting for the rest of the group. The benefit is threefold — the environment remains quiet, faster participants don't become bored waiting and slower participants are given the time they require to complete their postcards.

# SALE OF THE MINUTE

 **LEARNING OUTCOMES** A team review activity that includes 33 questions about the training course.

 **OVERVIEW** This fast-paced team review is based on the television show 'Sale of the Century'. Playing three rounds of 10 questions, teams beat the buzzer to answer correctly and accumulate points. Each round includes a 'fame game' board and an optional 'gift shop'.

 **IN MY EXPERIENCE...** This is an excellent end-of-day or end-of-course review activity for multi-day training courses that are rich in content.

 **THE HIDDEN TWIST** This is a disguised test of 33 questions. Participants display intense competitiveness and drive to win.

 **ESSENTIAL DATA**

| | |
|---|---|
| **COURSE TYPE** | Any |
| **GROUP SIZE** | 6–20 |
| **TIME OF DAY** | End-of-day or end-of-course review activity |
| **PACE** | Fast and competitive |
| **TIME TO CREATE** | 2–6 hours (depending on how elaborate you make the fame game board) |
| **TIME TO RUN** | 40 minutes |

 **STEPS TO CREATE**

1. Create three rounds of Sale of the Minute questions.
2. Each round should be structured as follows:
   - Questions 1–5
   - Fame game question, e.g. Who am I? Or What am I?
   - Questions 6–8
   - Gift Shop (optional; use promotional items, candy or other prizes)
   - Questions 9 and 10
3. Create a fame game board:
   - You will need to draw nine faces or symbols that relate to the course. For example, in credit management use Bill Invoice, Ann Accountant, Chris Credit, etc. In project management use Gary Gantt, Terri Timeline, Rich Resource, etc.

- Decide on which faces have prizes and which faces win. Round 1 = 1 face has $10, Round 2 = $15 is added behind another face, Round 3 = $25 is added behind another face. This can be recorded and kept by the trainer.
4. Create a tie-break question. A fourth Fame Game question will be required should two or more teams be at the same score at the end of the third round.
5. Create a gift shop scenario. For example, if you are selling a corporate T-shirt, your scenario may be: 'This excellent quality T-shirt proudly displays our company logo. It is made of high-quality polyester cotton made by Raccoon Inc, makers of T-shirts of distinction. Valued at $45, this T-shirt can be yours for $6'.
6. Collect noisemakers (rattle, drum, maracas, bells, etc.).
7. Collect prizes for gift shop. Ensure you have a prize for each player in the team. (It's pretty hard to split a T-shirt!)
8. Collect prizes for fame game.
9. Collect prizes for all players for the end of the game.
10. Create a scoreboard, with the heading Sale of the Minute

### STEPS TO RUN
1. Regroup to small groups (3–5 participants).
2. Have each group think of a team name. Write this name on a name plate or piece of paper on their table.
3. Explain the rules of the game:
   - Sale of the Minute has three rounds of 10 questions. Each round of questions also has a 'fame game' and a 'gift shop' element.
   - Each team begins with $20.
   - After each question is asked teams must beat the buzzer in order to get a chance to answer the question.
   - For each correct question +$5.
   - For each incorrect question -$5 and other teams can then answer.
   
   **FAME GAME:** As the 'Who am I' or 'What am I' is being read teams can 'buzz in' with answers. If they are correct they can choose from the fame game board.
   If not correct, then all remaining teams can answer at any time during the question.
   **GIFT SHOP:** For the highest-scoring team at that point.
4. Award prizes to the highest-scoring team and consolation prizes for all other players.

### SUGGESTED DEBRIEF STRATEGY/SAMPLE QUESTIONS

Take notice of any areas of learning in which participants are having difficulty and ensure that any gaps in their learning are filled before continuing with more content.

### SUGGESTED TRAINING COURSES

#### PROCESS IMPROVEMENT

Our process improvement training course is run over six days, as two-day segments over three to four weeks. Sale of the Minute is an excellent way to end each two-day segment. The participants carry their scores over from each week with the grand final being played during the last session. In a training course rich in content, Sale of the Minute provides the final climax for each segment of learning.

#### TEAM DEVELOPMENT

Sale of the Minute fosters team development. All players work as a team during the review activity. Questions on all areas of team development and the fame game board could include famous teams from history.

**TIPS, TRICKS AND TRAPS** The work to create this review activity will pay off in learning outcomes and participant enthusiasm. I create this review activity for training courses that are lengthy, rich in content and will be conducted several times. Remember, Sale of the Minute is a disguised test of 33 questions in a fun, team-based and energising way — in 40 minutes — that's a great use of training review time!

# SEQUENCE SHUFFLE

 **LEARNING OUTCOMES** To ensure that participants are confident in the correct sequence of a step-by-step procedure.

 **OVERVIEW** This is a 'physical form' of Step Mix. Participants are given cards bearing one step of a process. In a circle, they form the correct sequence of the steps. The trainer then has the opportunity of asking 'why' and 'what if' questions about the sequence.

 **IN MY EXPERIENCE...** From basic computer training, to the most advanced process improvement course, I have used sequence shuffle to great effect. Its kinesthetic nature allows participants to become part of the sequence, which heightens their retention.

 **THE HIDDEN TWIST** I have found that months later, participants remember not only their step in the sequence, but have better retention of the whole sequence of steps. Because they have been kinesthetically involved and can visualise where other participants have stood and their cards, they remember the step-by-step procedure better than just reading it in their participant manual.

 **ESSENTIAL DATA**

| | |
|---|---|
| **COURSE TYPE** | Any |
| **GROUP SIZE** | 4–12 |
| **TIME OF DAY** | Start-of-session, end-of-session or post-lunch activity |
| **PACE** | Moderate |
| **TIME TO CREATE** | 10–30 minutes |
| **TIME TO RUN** | 5–20 minutes |

 **STEPS TO CREATE**
1. Write the steps of a sequence (step-by-step procedure) on separate sheets of card (approximately A4 in size).
2. (**OPTIONAL:** Extra cards can be written with additional steps, incorrect steps or a blank card can be included, for which the group decides on the correct wording for the step.)
3. Have Blu Tac or masking tape to hand.

## STEPS TO RUN

1. Give participants one or two cards each (until all cards are used).
2. Have participants physically form the sequence.
3. Have them read their steps in the sequence. (I recommend reading the sequence aloud three times, increasing the enthusiasm and gusto each time!)
4. Put the cards on the wall using Blu Tac or masking tape.

## SUGGESTED DEBRIEF STRATEGY/SAMPLE QUESTIONS

- The trainer should ask 'why' and 'what if' questions to add depth to the learning.
- Selecting a participant: 'What would happen if we removed this step?'
- 'What other topics/processes/procedures are related to this step-by-step procedure?'
- 'Why is this step important?'
- 'What makes this step different from _____?'
- 'How can you apply this when you return to your job?'
- Selecting an incorrect card: 'What would happen if we added this step?'

## WORKING EXAMPLE

**COMPUTERS, PROCESS IMPROVEMENT, SELLING AND TRAIN THE TRAINER**

Select a sequence of steps that is traditionally difficult to remember.

**COMPUTER TRAINING**

In computer training include each specific keystroke step, e.g. 'press OK'.

**PROCESS IMPROVEMENT**

In process improvement, choose a process that generates discussion on the correct sequence, for example seeking approval for the deployment of a new process may involve some variation, depending on the project.

**SELLING SKILLS**

Target day-to-day processes of records management and client meetings.

**TRAIN THE TRAINER**

Sequences of course development, daily planning and the pre-course process would be suitable for 'sequence shuffle'.

**TIPS, TRICKS AND TRAPS** This review activity is deceptively simple. Participants often find it difficult to put a long process into sequence. The benefit is threefold — all participants are involved in the ordering, participants say their step/s out loud, the steps are put on the wall as a visual reminder.

# SQUAD CHALLENGE

 **LEARNING OUTCOMES** Participants review a section of a training course by creating their own questions to challenge opposing team/s.

 **OVERVIEW** In small groups participants create 10 questions or true/false statements. Each squad challenges other squads to answer. The aim is to stump the opposing squad.

 **IN MY EXPERIENCE...** No other review activity has participants as eager to look back through their resource material and participant guide to find the most difficult and tricky questions.

 **THE HIDDEN TWIST** Participants are so keen to create twists and tricks with the wording of questions or true/false statements that they rarely notice that they are doing the review for themselves!

 **ESSENTIAL DATA**

| | |
|---|---|
| **COURSE TYPE** | Any |
| **GROUP SIZE** | 4–12 |
| **TIME OF DAY** | Any time. Particularly good as a start-of-day review activity on the second or third day of a multi-day course. |
| **PACE** | Moderate |
| **TIME TO CREATE** | Negligible |
| **TIME TO RUN** | 35–45 minutes |

 **STEPS TO CREATE**
1. Have paper and pens for participants.
2. Prepare a tie-break or 'who am I' question.
3. Collect prizes for winning team and other players.

 **STEPS TO RUN**
1. Regroup into two groups.
2. Have each group:
   • Invent a squad name.
   • Create either 10 questions or 10 true/false statements. The aim is to stump the opposing squad.

- An answer sheet with the 10 answers on it is to be handed to the trainer (as the adjudicator).
3. Decide which team is to go first. That team asks their questions. The trainer keeps score.
4. Award prizes to the winning team and consolation prizes to all other players.

## SUGGESTED DEBRIEF STRATEGY/SAMPLE QUESTIONS
- During the review activity, the trainer should be aware of sections of content that are being omitted from the participant questions.
- Be prepared, in a tie break, to ask a question on a 'beat the buzzer' or 'who am I' basis.

## WORKING EXAMPLE
### BUSINESS WRITING
Business writing often contains lots of small yet important detail that participants revel in testing. For example, grammar, punctuation, sentence construction and report layout all provide ample opportunity for participants to develop detailed and tricky questions.

### CAREER DEVELOPMENT
True/false statements in career development might cover areas such as reflecting on your first job, job versus career skills versus talents versus interests, key attributes, job satisfaction and value and perception, and myths about poor jobs. In this concept-based course, which requires self-reflection, this activity reviews the more solid theory base.

**TIPS, TRICKS AND TRAPS** Keep the pace lively throughout the question phase of the review. Impose tight time limits on the groups for creating their questions of, say, 15 minutes.

# STEP MIX

**LEARNING OUTCOMES** To ensure that participants are confident in the correct sequence of a step-by-step procedure.

**OVERVIEW** Participants are given cards bearing a single step of a process. They place the cards on the training room wall in order. To add depth to the review two or more step-by-step processes can be jumbled up. The trainer then has the opportunity of asking 'why' and 'what if' questions about the sequence.

**IN MY EXPERIENCE...** This is one of the quickest and most basic yet effective ways to review a step-by-step process. Don't let the simplicity of the review put you off running it. I have conducted this review activity with all course topics and all levels of participants to great effect.

**THE HIDDEN TWIST** When two or more processes are mixed together the review becomes rather more difficult. Participants really have to work together to solve the puzzle.

**ESSENTIAL DATA**

| | |
|---|---|
| **COURSE TYPE** | Any |
| **GROUP SIZE** | 1–12 |
| **TIME OF DAY** | Start-of-session, end-of-session or post-lunch activity |
| **PACE** | Moderate |
| **TIME TO CREATE** | 10–30 minutes |
| **TIME TO RUN** | 5–20 minutes |

**STEPS TO CREATE**
1. Write the steps of a process (step-by-step procedure) on separate sheets of card (approximately A4 in size).
2. (**OPTIONAL:** Two or more processes can be mixed together: create heading cards for each process.)
3. Have Blu Tac or masking tape to hand.

## STEPS TO RUN

1. Give participants one or two cards each (until all cards are used).
2. Have participants form the step-by-step process.
3. Put the cards on the wall using Blu Tac or masking tape under heading cards (if appropriate).

## SUGGESTED DEBRIEF STRATEGY/SAMPLE QUESTIONS

- The trainer should ask 'why' and 'what if' questions to add depth to the learning.
- Selecting a participant: 'What would happen if we removed this step?'
- 'What other topics/processes/procedures are related to this step-by-step procedure?'
- 'Why is this step important?'
- 'What makes this step different from _____?'
- 'How can you apply this when you return to your job?'
- Selecting an incorrect card: 'What would happen if we added this step?'

## WORKING EXAMPLE

### CHANGE MANAGEMENT

If you are using a model of change management (for example: four steps, denial/resistance, exploration, adaptation, integration), these cards could be mixed with substeps for each of the four steps of the model. Participants not only have to order the four steps but each of the substeps as well.

### PERFORMANCE IMPROVEMENT

Step Mix might be used to consolidate how the performance improvement methodology needs to be implemented. Alternatively, if you are training a new performance management system, then you might review the steps to handling a specific performance scenario.

**TIPS, TRICKS AND TRAPS** This review activity is simple in design and in execution. The value of the review is twofold — the review itself and in the opportunity for a powerful debrief based on 'why' and 'what if' questions.

# TRUE/FALSE

 **LEARNING OUTCOMES** A whole-group review activity of 12 statements that are either true or false.

 **OVERVIEW** Participants sort cards of true or false statements into order and then engage in a whole-group discussion. This is a review activity that can be slotted into a training course for use almost anywhere during the day.

 **IN MY EXPERIENCE...** It is a rare course where I don't include a true/false review. This is also the kind of review activity that I create as a contingency measure to have on hand if I am running ahead of time.

 **THE HIDDEN TWIST** The learning in the review is in the debrief of both the true and the false statements. Give particular attention to the false statements, asking: 'what would make this true.'

 **ESSENTIAL DATA**

| | |
|---|---|
| **COURSE TYPE** | Any |
| **GROUP SIZE** | 1–12 |
| **TIME OF DAY** | Any time. Particularly good as start-of-session, end-of-session, post-lunch or overnight task. |
| **PACE** | Moderate |
| **TIME TO CREATE** | 30 minutes |
| **TIME TO RUN** | 15 minutes |

 **STEPS TO CREATE**
1. Write 12 statements, the answer being true or false onto cards or use Microsoft's PowerPoint to create each statement on a separate slide for printing.
2. Create two heading cards, true and false

 **STEPS TO RUN**
1. Handout cards to participants.
2. Have them work together to establish whether each statement is true or false and then put them on the wall under the appropriate heading.

3. When all participants have finished go through each statement. Go through false cards first.
   - If the answer is false, ask 'what would make this true?'
4. Read remaining true cards.
   - If the answer is true, ask 'why' and 'what if' questions to add depth to the learning.

## SUGGESTED DEBRIEF STRATEGY/SAMPLE QUESTIONS

- The trainer should ask 'why' and 'what if' questions to add depth to the learning.
  'What would make this true?'
  'What other topics are related here?'
  'Why is this important?'
  'What makes this statement different from _____?'
  'How can you apply this when you return to your job?'
  [for a false statement] 'What would happen if you did this?'

## WORKING EXAMPLE

### LEADERSHIP
This is an excellent review for a leadership course where physical activity is often required to break up theoretical or conceptual sessions.

### PROJECT MANAGEMENT
Where there is controversy about a statement, be sure to listen to the reasoning of both sides. For example, in project management training a statement of 'you should get preliminary sign-off of your project before benchmarking' may be neither true nor false, depending on the project. Listen to participants who think this is true and to those who think it is false. Hearing both sides of the discussion has positive effects for all participants.

**TIPS, TRICKS AND TRAPS** The trap that inexperienced trainers often fall into is not handling false answers well. Remember, there is no learning for participants in 'false'. In a review activity, we must embed the true answer in the participant's mind, not the false ones. Always ask 'what would make this statement true?' to ensure that participants know the correct approach.

# WORDFINDER

**LEARNING OUTCOMES** An individual activity that has participants search for keywords from the training course.

**OVERVIEW** Using a crossword maker or wordfinder computer software package, create a puzzle where the key terms of the course are hidden in the puzzle. Words can run horizontally, vertically, backwards or forwards. Usually the remaining letters will form a key term in the training course.

**IN MY EXPERIENCE...** This is a great activity as an overnight review. I also have a wordfinder on hand as a review for participants who perhaps complete an activity earlier than their classmates.

**THE HIDDEN TWIST** While this review is simply to find a word it is an opportunity to embed technical terms or business-specific terms.

**ESSENTIAL DATA**

| | |
|---|---|
| **COURSE TYPE** | Any |
| **GROUP SIZE** | 1–5 000 |
| **TIME OF DAY** | Any time. Particularly good as an overnight task. |
| **PACE** | Moderate |
| **TIME TO CREATE** | 1–2 hours |
| **TIME TO RUN** | 10–30 minutes |

**STEPS TO CREATE**
1. Write a list of key terms from the training course.
2. Using a computer software package, create the wordfinder puzzle.
3. Print as a handout for participants.
4. Print the answer sheet for the trainer.

**STEPS TO RUN**
1. Handout to participants.
2. Explain that the words listed below the puzzle are hidden in the puzzle. Words run horizontally, vertically, backwards and forwards.
3. After participants have finished ask further questions on technical terms, business-specific terms and acronyms that have been included in the puzzle.

## SUGGESTED DEBRIEF STRATEGY/SAMPLE QUESTIONS

• The trainer should ask 'why' and 'what if' questions to add depth to the learning.
  'What other topics are related here?'
  'Why is this important?'

## WORKING EXAMPLE

### INDUCTION

This is an excellent review for induction training that most likely has business-specific terminology included and acronyms that are commonly used within the organisation.

### QUALITY

Quality courses can often include slogans or sayings such as 'walking the talk' or 'quality counts', which can be included in a wordfinder puzzle along with other quality terms such as variation, data, vendors, statistical, shrink and guess.

### TEAM DEVELOPMENT

In team development training, I have used this review as a team-based activity. Print two large wordfinder puzzles and turn the review into a race. The first team to find all of the words wins!

**TIPS, TRICKS AND TRAPS** This review activity would be a nightmare to design without a computer software package to help you. These can be purchased inexpensively in the games section of your computer retailer or downloaded from the Internet. Most crossword makers also include a wordfinder puzzle.

# CHAPTER NINE

## DEBRIEFING
## A REVIEW

* WHY IS DEBRIEFING THE CRUCIAL STEP?

* HOW TO FRAME DEBRIEFING QUESTIONS

* FEEDBACK — NOT FAILURE

# WHAT IS A DEBRIEF?

A debrief is conducted by the trainer as the final step to the review activity. During the debrief the trainer checks learning, fills any remaining gaps in learning and ensures that participants are confident about moving on to the next session of learning.

# WHY IS DEBRIEFING THE CRUCIAL STEP?

Learning is evolutionary. Knowledge and learning is formed step by step and over time. During a training session the participant should become proficient with each stage of the learning, gaining the confidence to progress to further stages. A review activity builds a strong first step to boost the participant's confidence in their new skills and knowledge.

The trainer must mediate in order for these things to happen. If left to themselves, only truly self-motivated participants will link the learning to real life and persist with applying their learning to their day-to-day lives. During the debrief, the trainer gives participants an opportunity to talk through their experience of the review activity and then discuss how they will transfer their learnings to their day-to-day lives.

The story in Chapter 7 about the tick-in-the-box trainer who didn't involve themselves or debrief the review activities also illustrates how participants, if left, will go with the flow of the course. In this example, the trainer simply asked, 'How did you go with that?', to which the participants replied, 'Good.' The trainer responded, 'Good' and moved on to the next topic. Even though the participants were adults, some highly qualified with a wealth of business experience, the unsafe learning environment created by this unskilled trainer was such that participants preferred to discuss their problems with each other on breaks than with the trainer in the training room.

If there is no debrief, there are potential issues and problems for the trainer. Here are a few problems and hidden issues that inexperienced trainers face when they make the decision (consciously or unconsciously) to skip a debrief:

- *The trainer can't be sure that participants are confident about moving on.* Participants who are confident about their knowledge of a topic and who have shown that they know will be happy to learn more. Participants who are not confident and need more practice or help with areas of their learning will struggle with more information. If this problem persists it will compound, often resulting in a participant eventually shutting down to even the simplest things. At this point the participant may say things like 'I just don't get it'. This frustration could be avoided by early correction and feedback from the trainer before the compounding effect comes into play.

- *The trainer does not know how participants felt during the review activity.* Were the participants confident, engaged, struggling, secure, positive, hard working? Did they struggle with a specific point? We know that people's emotional response has a direct impact on retention of new skills and knowledge. Furthermore, how can a trainer be sure that participants are emotionally secure and confident to return to their day-to-day working environment to apply their learning when the trainer doesn't check on participants' emotional state while in the training room? It's an enigma!

- *The trainer devalues the training course.* Remember those occasions at school when you did your homework and the next day the teacher didn't even ask for it? Remember when you gave the teacher an essay that you had worked hard on and the teacher gave you a mark with no comment — not even a correction anywhere? When trainers move on without debriefing an activity, participants may wonder what the point was of doing the review activity in the first place.

- *The trainer misses the opportunity to fill gaps in learning before moving on to the next topic.* Careful questioning, which adds depth to the review activity, is vital for a trainer to be absolutely certain that no gaps in learning remain before proceeding with the next part of the course. A good debrief sends a strong message to participants that 'this is your course' and that the trainer has taken the responsibility to ensure that participants are confident about their learning every step of the way. Participants begin to see that their learning is a partnership between themselves and the trainer.

- *The trainer misses the opportunity to build rapport* with participants, showing that they are genuinely interested in the participants and their learning.

## USING THE POWER OF THE GROUP

Participants need to know that they know for themselves, just as much as the trainer needs to know that they know. In his book, *Influence:Science and Practice*, Robert Cialdini discusses the notion of social proof. If a group of people have something, or think something, then others will naturally begin to follow or at least enquire about this social shift. Examples of this most basic social influence pattern can be seen throughout society in fashion, religion, housing trends, holiday destinations, patronising of restaurants and purchasing of brand names.

Social proof can be a powerful ally for a trainer too. During a debrief session participants talk openly about their successes with a review activity and the learning that has developed from it. An environment of positive social proof is created in which participants listen to the views of others and solve problems and issues together. They then move on to the next topic in a positive and confident state of mind.

In contrast with this, social proof can work against a trainer as well. For example, if the trainer has unwittingly created an unsafe learning environment in which it is not acceptable for participants to ask questions and seek clarification on their learning, then we see destructive social proof taking place.

It only takes a few participants who are struggling with the course and who are not being supported to begin an army of critics at coffee breaks ready for an assault during the next session. The assault might be verbalised and it might not. Either way, the army of critics has been marshalled and it will no doubt spread its message like disgruntled customers.

The point is, the professional trainer can't afford not to ensure that participants are confident with their learning every step of the way.

## THE BUILDING BLOCKS — QUESTIONS

Effective questioning is probably the single most important skill that professional trainers need in order to build two-way communication between themselves and their group. If the trainer lacks advanced questioning skills the training course becomes a mere presentation, a one-way transfer of information.

Sometimes, during a debrief session questions can be quite basic and closed, requiring only a yes or no or some other short factual answer. These questions are extremely straightforward, involve no depth of thought or ideas and imply nothing. If the trainer uses these questions they remain in the spotlight and the group is unlikely to open up. However, the power of the debrief is revealed when a trainer asks higher-order questions that call for elaborate answers, requiring examples and details appropriate to the situation. When a trainer uses higher-order questions, the group is forced to reflect and think about its learning and is more likely to engage in a richer conversation.

FIGURE 9.1 BASIC VERSUS HIGHER-ORDER QUESTIONS

| BASIC QUESTION | HIGHER-ORDER QUESTION |
|---|---|
| • WHAT DOES THIS REMIND YOU OF? | • HOW DOES THIS REMIND YOU OF SOMETHING THAT YOU ALREADY KNOW? |
| • DO YOU THINK THAT THIS IS A GOOD IDEA? | • WHAT MAKES THIS A GOOD IDEA? |
| • DO YOU HAVE ANY QUESTIONS? | • WHAT QUESTIONS ARE RAISED BY THIS ACTIVITY? |

## THE THREE-PHASE DEBRIEF

As a basic strategy for debriefing review activities, the following three-phase approach has been proven to besuccessful at encouraging open discussion about what happened during the review and how participants felt. The last phase is an important step during which participants summarise their learnings and link them to intended real-life applications.

## PHASE 1: WHAT HAPPENED?

The first phase of the review activity is to check what happened. Whether the review activity is an individual, paired, small-group or whole-group activity, it is important that participants articulate what happened in their own words. Even if the trainer feels that their vantage point gives them a clearer understanding of what happened, it is still simply a perception, so it is imperative to have participants convey their perceptions of what happened.

**FIGURE 9.2** // QUESTIONS ON WHAT HAPPENED FOR PARTICIPANTS?

| BASIC QUESTION | HIGHER-ORDER QUESTION |
|---|---|
| • WHAT HAPPENED? | • BEING AS SPECIFIC AS POSSIBLE, CAN YOU TELL ME WHAT HAPPENED DURING THE ACTIVITY? |
| • WHAT WENT WELL? | • WHAT DID YOU DO WELL DURING THIS ACTIVITY? |
| • WHAT WENT WRONG? | • IF YOU HAD TO DO THIS ACTIVITY AGAIN, WHAT WOULD YOU DO DIFFERENTLY NEXT TIME? |
| • IS THIS A NEW IDEA? | • HOW DOES THIS LINK TO OTHER TOPICS WE HAVE COVERED SO FAR? |

## PHASE 2: HOW DID YOU FEEL?

So that they can move forward to implementing their learnings, participants should express or personally reflect on their emotional state as the bridging phase between phase 1 'What happened?' and phase 3 'What did you learn?'.

**FIGURE 9.3** // QUESTIONS ON HOW PARTICIPANTS FELT?

| BASIC QUESTION | HIGHER-ORDER QUESTION |
|---|---|
| • HOW DID YOU FEEL? | • HOW DID THE [ACTIVITY] HELP OR HINDER YOU? |
| • ARE YOU CONFIDENT ABOUT THESE NEW SKILLS? | • IF YOU HAD TO RATE YOURSELF ON A CONFIDENCE SCALE BETWEEN ZERO AND 10 (0 = ZERO CONFIDENCE, 10 = FULLY CONFIDENT), WHAT SCORE WOULD YOU GIVE YOURSELF? WHY? |
| • WHAT DO YOU THINK OF THIS NEW IDEA? | • WHAT WAS YOUR FIRST THOUGHT ON THIS NEW IDEA? WHAT ARE YOUR THOUGHTS NOW? |

## PHASE 3: WHAT DID YOU LEARN?

Without the vital step of linking the activity to key learnings, you leave the participants at risk of wondering whether the activity had any point. A solid debrief strategy sees the trainer asking questions to elicit key learning points, fill remaining gaps and ensure that participants are ready to apply their learning.

**FIGURE 9.4** // QUESTIONS TO ESTABLISH KEY LEARNING POINTS

| BASIC QUESTION | HIGHER-ORDER QUESTION |
|---|---|
| • WHAT DIDN'T YOU LEARN? | • WHAT ELSE DO YOU WANT TO KNOW ABOUT THIS TOPIC? |
| • WHAT DID YOU LEARN? | • CAN YOU SUMMARISE YOUR LEARNING IN ONE SENTENCE? |

FIGURE 9.5 // QUESTIONS TO IDENTIFY LEARNING GAPS

| BASIC QUESTION | HIGHER-ORDER QUESTION |
|---|---|
| • DO YOU HAVE ANY QUESTIONS? | • WHAT QUESTIONS ARE RAISED BY THIS ACTIVITY? |
| • WHAT DOES THIS REMIND YOU OF? | • HOW DOES THIS REMIND YOU OF SOMETHING THAT YOU ALREADY KNOW? |
| • ARE THEIR ANY GAPS IN YOUR LEARNING? | • WHAT ELSE DO YOU NEED TO KNOW BEFORE YOU CAN APPLY YOUR LEARNING? |

FIGURE 9.6 // QUESTIONS TO GAIN PARTICIPANTS' COMMITMENT TO APPLYING THEIR LEARNING

| BASIC QUESTION | HIGHER-ORDER QUESTION |
|---|---|
| • DO YOU THINK THAT THIS IS A GOOD IDEA? | • WHAT MAKES THIS A GOOD IDEA? |
| • CAN YOU USE THIS IDEA? | • HOW CAN YOU USE THIS IDEA TOMORROW? |
| • HOW WILL YOU USE THIS? | • HOW WOULD YOU LIKE TO USE THIS AGAIN? WHY? |
| • HOW WILL YOU USE THIS? | • CAN YOU DESCRIBE A NEW APPLICATION FOR THIS IDEA? |
| • HOW WILL YOU USE THIS? | • WHY ARE YOU LEARNING THIS? [ANSWER WILL FIRST ADDRESS PARTICIPANT'S NEEDS, THEN MOVE TO APPLICATION] |
| • WHERE CAN YOU USE THIS IDEA? | • WHAT ARE THE POSSIBILITIES AND PROBABILITIES OF USING THIS IDEA? |
| • CAN YOU ORGANISE THIS INFORMATION DIFFERENTLY? | • HOW MIGHT YOU RE-ORGANISE THIS INFORMATION SO YOU CAN USE IT? |
| • WILL YOU HAVE PROBLEMS USING THIS NEW IDEA? | • WHAT ARE THE BARRIERS? HOW WILL YOU FEEL WHEN YOU ARE USING THIS NEW IDEA? |
| • ARE YOU GOING TO USE THIS NEW SKILL? | • SO THAT YOU CAN PUT THIS IDEA INTO ACTION, WHAT IS THE NEXT STEP? WHAT ARE THE REMAINING STEPS? |
| • WHAT WILL YOU DO TO REACH YOUR GOAL? | • WHAT MILESTONES AND CRITICAL ELEMENTS NEED TO FEATURE IN YOUR PLAN FOR YOU TO REACH YOUR GOAL? |

# FEEDBACK NOT FAILURE!

The successful trainer encourages participants to remember that the important thing is not always to be right — the training room represents an opportunity to learn. If the fruit of the tree is out on a limb you are bound to fall off regularly! In review activities, progress often comes with risk, and risk inevitably means failure some of the time. Participants and trainers alike should understand that failures are only temporary setbacks.

## BUILDING A PARTNERSHIP FOR LEARNING

The building of partnerships between trainer and participants during a training course is a great goal to have as a trainer. This way, participants understand that you are genuinely interested in their development and know that they are responsible for their own learning. If there is a true partnership between trainer and participants throughout the training course, the debrief of a review activity is seen as positive encouragement of the participants' learning and a guiding hand to ensure that the learning is applied in their day-to-day lives. Similarly, participants are more willing to seek advice and act on it. Furthermore, if a partnership develops between participants, the debrief session becomes richer still because participants are correcting each other and all the answers aren't coming from the trainer.

## TAKING FEEDBACK FROM THE GROUP

As trainers, we expect participants to take our feedback constructively and unemotionally. And as trainers, we must also abide by this rule. If we expect to give feedback that is aimed at the positive development of others, then we must also accept feedback about our own training techniques.

For example, during a debrief, questions may be raised by one or a few of the group on a particular topic and the upshot may be that the group detects what they see as a gap in the training. An inexperienced trainer may quickly jump to their own defence with words such as 'As I said before…' or, with a sigh, 'I've been over this three times now…'. The professional trainer patiently unravels the issue and then, if necessary, retrains the topic using a different approach to ensure that all participants are confident. The professional trainer also learns from this experience and, after the course, refines their teaching of that topic and so continuously improves.

## USING THE 'WHAT IF' AND 'WHY' LINES OF QUESTIONING

Bernice McCarthy's 4-Mat model describes two types of learners who are often forgotten —'why learners' and 'what if learners'. An ideal opportunity to accommodate these learning types is during the debrief of a review activity. Simply by using questions starting with 'why' and 'what if', trainers can probe into content areas and stretch participants' understanding further than they could with the basic 'what' and 'how' teaching style.

### *A working example*

For example, suppose you were the trainer of a course on teamwork and had just conducted a true/false activity. The review activity covered topics such as core concepts of teams, working in teams, communicating within your team and so on. A few of the many questions that may be asked by the trainer could include:

**FIGURE 9.7** // TEAMWORK TRAINING

DEBRIEF QUESTIONS AFTER A TRUE/FALSE REVIEW ACTIVITY

| CATEGORY OF TRUE/FALSE STATEMENT | EXAMPLE OF A QUESTION TO BUILD KNOWLEDGE |
|---|---|
| QUALITY | • WHY IS IT IMPORTANT FOR YOUR TEAM TO BE KNOWLEDGEABLE ON QUALITY ISSUES?<br>• WHAT IF QUALITY CONTROL IS NOT PART OF YOUR TEAM'S MISSION? |
| TEAMS AND TIME | • WHY IS TIME MANAGEMENT LINKED TO YOUR TEAM'S OVERALL IMPROVEMENT? |
| MULTI-SKILLING | • WHAT IF YOUR TEAM IS NOT MULTI-SKILLED?<br>• WHAT MIGHT BE DIFFERENT IF YOUR TEAM GOT MORE AND BETTER TRAINING? |
| TEAM LEADERSHIP | • WHAT IF YOUR TEAM HAD NO LEADER?<br>• WHY IS LEADERSHIP BETTER SHARED? |
| TEAM REVIEWS | • WHY DOES YOUR TEAM CONTINUALLY NEED PERFORMANCE REVIEWS?<br>• WHAT MIGHT HAPPEN IF YOUR TEAM BECAME COMPLACENT ABOUT THEIR LEVEL OF PERFORMANCE? |

# AT THE END OF THE DEBRIEF

Learning logs or learning journals written during the training course relate to the learning at hand. Learning logs may be separate booklets used specifically and solely for logging key learning points or they may be part of a participant workbook.

## USING A LEARNING LOG OR LEARNING JOURNAL

Learning logs are a wonderful tool to use as part of a debrief following a review activity. The key to learning logs is that the participants' learning is linked from the first moment to its future application in their day-to-day lives. For example, after a review activity has been debriefed, participants might be asked to record their key learning points in their learning log and then write down how they intend to apply those learnings in their day-to-day work.

The procedure for using learning logs begins with the introduction of the tool to participants early in the training course. At various intervals during the course (at least twice each day), give participants time to update their learning log. This process takes only about 10 minutes, and it solidifies knowledge and builds commitment to implementing learnings via an action plan. For more information on how to create a learning log or journal, refer to Chapter 8.

## SUMMARY

- During the debrief the trainer checks learning, fills any remaining gaps in learning and ensures participants are confident about moving on to the next session of learning.
- If the trainer leaves the debrief process out of the review activity, they can't be sure that participants are confident about moving on, they don't know the participants' emotional state and this devalues the training course. The trainer also misses the opportunity to fill gaps in learning and build rapport with participants.
- Effective questioning is probably the single most important skill that a professional trainer needs in order to build two-way communication between themselves and their group.
- Basic questions should be transformed into high-order questions that call for elaborate answers, examples and a depth of treatment appropriate to the situation.
- The three phases of a debrief are 1. What happened? 2. How did you feel, and 3. What did you learn?
- Debriefing a review activity further cements the partnership between the trainer and the participants.
- 'Why' and 'what if' questions help to delve into learning and expand the process of understanding.

Debriefing and other post-course measures help to maximise the impact of training and the application of the skills learnt. Those trainers who conduct post-course measures know the effort required, but they can see that it is an integral part of their role. However, there are many trainers who just say good-bye at the door and never speak to their participants again! Some of the review activities in Chapter 8 will help you to conduct post-course reviews which can be sent to participants after the training to sustain their learning.

# CHAPTER TEN

## TIPS AND TRICKS

* NO TIME FOR PREPARATION?

* A QUALITY COURSE ON A LOW BUDGET?

* CREATIVITY BLOCK?

# KEYS TO SUCCESS

The single most common lament I hear from professional trainers worldwide is that they don't have enough time to prepare training courses. For most trainers gone are the days of development ratios of 40:1 (40 days of preparation and development for each day of training). In the constantly changing workplace, trainers are now expected to produce high quality training materials quickly and conduct training that works.

Flexibility and good organisation are two keys for success. A trainer who remains flexible in their approach to training will be happy to take components from one course and add them to another, like building blocks of learning. The second key is good organisation. Too often trainers re-invent the wheel by redoing training materials or training activities that they have lost owing to poor organisation. An organised logistics area where activities and materials are stored and a good computerised filing system are essential for fast turnaround on instructional design and course development.

If your logistics and computers are a bit of a mess or you have limited time, no budget or are feeling stressed, then read on. The following points should help you to get your life in order quickly (when it comes to training review activities that is!).

## USE REVIEW ACTIVITIES THAT REQUIRE NO PREPARATION

No time for preparation? Then use review activities that require no preparation.

- A sensational start-of-day review activity is Squad Challenge. It requires no organisation on your part and I know of no better review activity for getting participants poring over every page of their participant workbook/reference guide searching for trick questions to stump the opposing team.
- A review for after lunch requiring nothing from the trainer is Hot Tips. Give participants a piece of coloured paper and have them write down their key learnings from the morning session. Then have them write down how they will apply their learnings in their day-to-day lives. Toss a stress ball (or other soft ball) randomly from participant to participant asking for their Hot Tips and how they will apply them. All this for zero preparation on your part!
- A great end-of-day review activity is Gallery of Learning. Give participants a piece of flip-chart paper and some pens and have them create a poster of their key learnings and then present it to the group. This review starts off as a reflective activity — participants analyse key points — and then turns into a high-energy presentation from each group.

## BUILD REVIEWS YOU CAN USE ENDLESSLY

Try designing reviews you can use time and again without recreating them.

Board games are wonderful additions to a trainer's library of activities. I have about 15 board games in my logistics cupboard that we have created over the past few years.

Regardless of the topic I am training, I can quickly write some questions and 'hey presto', it looks like I've been preparing for weeks! This allows me to produce or customise a training course quickly and, just as quickly, slot in professional-looking review activities.

- Invest in high-quality review activities of business-specific models. For example, we once created a foam cutout of a three-tiered pyramid model used in a number of sales training courses. This model can be used to teach and to review and will never wear out. The trainer always looks prepared and professional. Other learning aids we have devised have been giant jigsaws of models or key learning points. They make fantastic review activities and will last forever. Investing in these 'training assets' rewards both trainers and participants.
- Laminate the cards you use during review activities. For example, true/false cards or definition match cards are unlikely to change over time. If you invest in a laminating machine or the cost of having it done you will be repaid in time saved.
- Turn the spotlight onto participants. Instead of you doing all the work, get them to create questions, true/false statements or fill-in-the-gaps puzzles to stump their opponents in other teams. There is as much, if not more, learning in creating questions as in answering them.
- Keep a filing system of review activities. Often a review activity is based on a generic handout that can be used regardless of the topic. For example, Hot Tips can be used for any training course. Keep a general-purpose file stocked with copies for you to grab when you are rushing against deadlines.

## STRATEGIES FOR LOW BUDGETS
So you have no budget, but you still have to produce a high-quality course?

- Choose paper and pen type activities. Amazing review activities come from coloured cardboard and coloured markers.
- Never pass a discount store without going in. So-called 'junk shops' are full of ideas for trainers. An endless array of stickers, containers, household items, party gear and games can be adapted for use in good solid review activities. With some creativity and innovation you can create marvellous activities that will produce great learning outcomes. The key to success is don't limit your ideas!
- Borrow! If you see another trainer conducting a review activity you like, ask to borrow the idea. Many trainers have called on us when they are in a tight spot and we have loaned them a board game or have quickly created something for them to use in review activities.
- Build up a library. Never throw anything out. Keep a logistics cupboard/s that neatly house all of your review activities. Ensure that after you use an activity it is tidy and ready to go for next time. Purchase new or repair broken moving devices or noisemakers, remake damaged question cards.

## TRAINER'S BLOCK

You may have experienced a block in creativity or even felt that you don't have what it takes to design review activities.

- You don't have to be creative. What you need to be is focussed on your goals. Identify key learning messages that participants must know and work that content into a process by which you can measure whether or not your participants know these key content areas.
- Cheat! 'Cheating' simply means getting your ideas from many different sources. The first source is this book. Use its activities to help you create your own review activities. The second source is other trainers. They will often help you to be creative. Sometimes, as the writer of a training course, I am simply too close to the content to be creative with process. Other trainers can help. The third source of ideas is other books and people not directly involved in training. Use books on games, activities and party themes for children to spark ideas on how they can be woven into a review activity for adults. Ask work colleagues, friends and family to help you. Sometimes, simply talking through the content with someone else allows you to take the next step and, with that person's help, create an activity that measures the learning concerned.

## DEALING WITH STRESS

It is not easy to have to prepare a training course while you are feeling stressed.

Relieve your stress, then write your training course. A trainer once told us at a session I attended that 'prepared trainers come from prepared lives'. We know that stress levels affect creativity, speed of work, tone of voice, accuracy and many other aspects vital to creating excellent training sessions. If you are embarking on writing a training course you need to establish what is the best use of your available time. This may mean that you allocate some time to ensuring that your home life is ordered, having a massage, taking a walk in a nearby park, going to the gym or something else that relieves tension. Investing time in relieving stress before you start writing your training course will pay huge dividends in effectiveness and overall productivity as you strive to meet your training goals.

## SUMMARY

- Be flexible and organised. If you are you will always be open to new ideas, able to meet tight deadlines and innovative about finding the materials you need.
- If you have limited time to prepare, use review activities that require little or no preparation. Make sure you are able to reuse review activities that do take time to prepare by laminating cards and storing with care.
- Make the necessary investment in creating 3D models and board games. These can be used endlessly and in many different training courses. You will always look

prepared — even at a moment's notice!

- If you have a limited budget, use paper and pen type activities. Use discount stores for logistics and borrow from other trainers. Most important, never throw anything out and be organised so that you can find things easily.

- If you are in the creativity doldrums, borrow ideas from other trainers, this book, friends and colleagues. People are usually willing to help — you just have to ask!

- Prepared trainers come from prepared lives. Relieve your stress before you prepare your training course. Investing some time in relieving stress before you begin will pay huge dividends in effectiveness and overall productivity as you strive to meet your training goals.

# EPILOGUE

I still travel across the Sydney Harbour Bridge regularly. Since the 2000 Olympic Games in Sydney and the improvements they occasioned for the road system the trip home seems quicker. However, time in traffic still provides me with the opportunity to reflect on my day, plus catch up on my phone calls.

Just last week, I was approaching the Sydney Harbour Bridge on my way to the airport to catch a flight to Auckland, New Zealand, where I was to conduct a training session. I checked the weather reading displayed on a North Sydney building — 28°C — perfect! How could I be leaving this fabulous weather? My car phone rang. I was pleased to hear the voice of Andrea, a trainer I had trained two years before. Andrea began training in her capacity as a human resources manager. At that time she was unsure about how she would juggle her already busy job with the new responsibility of training. Andrea was a participant at my Train the Trainer course and then at my Train the Trainer Master Class. It turned out that not only was Andrea good at training, but she really enjoyed it too. I hadn't heard from her for over 12 months.

Andrea was bursting with excitement. She said, 'I just had to call you.' From the tone of her voice, I thought she must have just won a lottery. 'Yesterday I finished a training course in our new performance management system. Last night in the middle of the night I woke up and the penny dropped about what training is about!' she went on.

Approaching the entrance to the Harbour Tunnel, I paid the toll while asking Andrea to tell me more about her 'penny drop'.

She explained, 'I realised for the first time since I began training two years ago that, I think, I just conducted a really good training course.'

Andrea went on to explain that she had consciously decided before the course that she was not going to be in the spotlight all the time. The aim of the performance management system training course was to show her managers the new format of the system and give them an opportunity to test-drive the process. Instead of doing her usual 'chalk and talk' routine of going through the forms, the computer system and the role-plays, she allowed participants to experiment with the process and simply be guided through it by her. In the two-day training course she conducted 12 review activities, finishing off with what she described as a hilarious Sale of the Minute review. 'I was concerned that my questions would be too difficult. I wrote them when I was cross with my manager — they were really tough. But, the participants were intensely competitive. At one point I split the points in half — each team got $2.50 — just to move on with the review! I was laughing so much I could hardly read the fame game question!', Andrea said.

I asked Andrea about the feedback from the course. 'It was fantastic. I have never seen evaluation forms with so much written on them.' She went on, 'The participants had learnt so much and I knew that they knew!'

I was now as thrilled as she was. I asked her how she felt about this milestone. She thought for a moment and then, in a reflective tone, said, 'I feel like a real trainer.' Her voice quickened again, 'I feel like I made a difference and that each participant in my group is confident, no, really confident, with the new system and how to conduct a performance appraisal. They were all convinced our system is a good one that will make their jobs as managers easier and allow the feedback process to work. Usually, there is tonnes of baggage about every new system — but not this time. I think it was because we kept ironing out the little problems along the way. The confidence of the whole group never wavered and their energy levels remained high throughout the course.'

'Andrea, how difficult was it to do what you did?', I asked.

Andrea replied, 'Looking back to before the last two days, I would have thought this outcome would never have been possible. Truth be told, I did have a change in attitude and a change in my whole approach to training. This new way of thinking freed me up to explore how easy it actually is. I remember your Master Class session on review activities and taking responsibility for the participants' learning. That's what I focused on for the whole course.'

Andrea continued, 'At the end of my training courses, I used to go home, lie on the couch and have a glass of wine, watch TV and then promptly fall asleep. My partner always schedules a night out when I train — can't stand me. For the last two nights, I haven't felt tired at all. That has been an amazing thing for me, I actually feel good. Throughout the training course I was managing to do more for the participants without draining my own energy!'

Andrea's enthusiasm was great to hear. She had passed a huge milestone in training. Andrea was now a professional trainer who could confidently measure learning success while participants were in the training room.

After I returned from New Zealand, I received an email from Andrea.

## ⬩ EMAIL

**TO: CATHERINE MATTISKE**

**FROM: ANDREA RICKETT**

*Hi Catherine*

*Hope your trip to Auckland was great and that your training went well.*

*Attached are some emails that I received that I know you would love to see. I have done another course since I spoke with you and had another great result – it seems that I am on a roll! I am finding that I am fitting more into my training days and my last group of participants just powered through. Also, I am feeling far less stressed about training and I manage to not fall asleep on the couch after my training day.*

*It is great to get the feedback from participants and my manager – but I have to tell you – it is ME who is thrilled the most!*

*It was great to be able to share my excitement with someone who knows...*

*Andrea*

## ⬩ EMAIL

**TO: ANDREA RICKETT**

**FROM: ANTHONY KEHER (A PARTICIPANT ON ANDREA'S TRAINING COURSE)**

*Hi Andrea*

*I just wanted to drop you a line to tell you that I thought the Performance Management System training was fantastic. As you know, I was due to see my first direct report, Mark, today and it went really well. I managed to remember all the steps and what to do with all of the forms - I didn't even have to look at my reference guide! I have the other meetings scheduled for the next few days and for the first time, I am looking forward to conducting performance appraisals.*

*Also, my manager, Jennifer and I were discussing the whole Performance Management System. I showed her what we did in the course – she is booked in for your next class. Jennifer is keen for you to do a follow-up training session for all the managers on some more feedback techniques when dealing with some specific performance issues that we have here in our division. Can you do this for us?*

*Anyway, thanks again. It was the best course I have done. And by the way, Paul's team cheated – we should have got their $2.50 in the final review!*

*Regards*

*Anthony*

## ⬩ EMAIL

**TO: TIM WOO (ANDREA'S MANAGER)**

**FROM: ANDREA RICKETT**

**ATTACHED: COPY OF EMAIL ABOVE FROM**

*Hi Tim*

*Anthony just sent this feedback about my Performance Management System training that I ran last week. Thought you would like to read it!*

*Andrea*

## EMAIL

**TO: ANDREA RICKETT**
**FROM: TIM WOO (ANDREA'S MANAGER)**
**REGARDING ANTHONY'S FEEDBACK**

*Andrea,*

*Thanks for this great feedback. That's not the only feedback I've had. Several managers had stopped me in the corridor or said in meetings how wonderful your training was. Not only from Anthony's course but the last one as well. Well done! Whatever you are doing in these courses is working, keep it up. Maybe you can share with the other trainers at our next trainers meeting what you have done to get such great results?*

*I would like to discuss Anthony's request for further training. This is great. Anthony's boss Jennifer is not keen on her staff spending time on training – so her request is a terrific boost for all of us. I have scheduled a meeting tomorrow with you – it's in your Outlook Calendar. I'd like you to write the training course and if you have the time to run it. Anyway, let's have a preliminary chat about the content tomorrow.*

*Keep up the great work*

*Tim*

## IN CLOSING...

When concluding one of my training courses I use the magic colouring book that I found years ago in a tiny magic shop in Melbourne. Once, when I was training in Melbourne, I lost my magic book. To my delight the concierge at my hotel arranged for another to be delivered within the hour from — you guessed it — the same little magic shop. Not only was I relieved that I could run my training according to plan, I was handed a fabulous story for my next customer service training course. Now, many other trainers also use the magic colouring book as part of their training. Even though it is a popular 'training tool', I continue to use it. When you open the book for the first time all you see are blank pages. When you open it a second time, as if by magic, outlined drawings, like those in a colouring book, appear. The third time you open it, fully coloured pictures appear. If you open it again, the pages are blank again. It's simply magic. The story that I tell using the magic colouring book is a bit like a trainer using this book for the first time.

Allow me to relate the magic colouring book to the book in your hands, *Train for Results*.

When you purchased this book the term 'review activity' might have been just like a blank book for you — a brand new concept. You might have been training without truly understanding the importance of review and how it impacts on you, your participants and the organisation for which they work. You might have even recognised the importance, yet never really understood how to create and conduct review activities.

In this book, I have outlined the importance of review activities and the responsibility incumbent on professional trainers by giving you some direction and guidance — a bit like giving you a line drawing. However, it is only with practice and your own brand of application that you will be able to successfully create your versions of the review activities — a bit like a completely coloured-in drawing or being the artist of your own original creation.

However, without practice and continuous reflection your learning and hard work towards owning the concept of review activities could be lost — you could be back to a blank colouring book.

Once you have read this book, I would ideally like you, and all professional trainers, to move forward beyond the boundaries and guidelines that I have given you here. I hope that each professional trainer will create their own unique collection of review activities — their own works of art. Once this new way of conducting training courses, with an integral process of 'knowing they know', becomes part of their regular work as a trainer, the accolades from participants and those representing organisations won't be very far behind.

Finally, it is my fervent hope that trainers take the time to reflect on and applaud their own work. After all, true artists don't need public acclaim, they find satisfaction in the knowledge that their work is the best it can be and that they have set a new and higher standard.

## REFERENCES

Cialdini, R. B. 2001. *Influence: Science and Practice*. Allyn and Bacon, Boston, MA.

De Bono, E. 1994. *Parallel Thinking: From Socratic Thinking to De Bono Thinking*. Viking. London.

Gardner, H. 1985. *Frames of Mind: The Theory of Multiple Intelligences*. Basic Books, New York.

Goleman, D. 1995. *Emotional Intelligence*. Bantam Books, New York.

McCarthy, B. 1996. *About Learning*. Excel, Barrington, Ill.

| | | |
|---|---|---|
| WHAT IS THE BENEFIT OF BEING ASSERTIVE? | WHAT IS ONE DISADVANTAGE OF BEING PASSIVE? | WHAT ARE THE 3 TYPES OF BEHAVIOUR? |
| WHO IS THE AUTHOR OF THE WIN–WIN MODEL? | WHAT IS A BENEFIT OF USING 'I STATEMENTS'? | NAME 4 TYPES OF BODY LANGUAGE? |
| WHAT IS THE THIRD STEP OF THE 4–STEP ASSERTIVE COMMUNICATION MODEL? | WHAT IS ONE THING YOU WILL DO TOMORROW TO APPLY YOUR LEARNINGS? | CAN YOU DEMONSTRATE SITTING IN AN AGGRESSIVE STYLE? |
| REWORD TO ASSERTIVE LANGUAGE: YOU MAKE ME FEEL SO UPSET? | REWORD TO ASSERTIVE LANGUAGE: CAN I TROUBLE YOU TO TAKE THIS TO PETER? | (HIDE THIS SHEET!) SPELL AGGRESSIVE |

| | | | | |
|---|---|---|---|---|
| ANNUAL REPORT | EVERY TWO YEARS | TO INFLUENCE | WRITER'S NAME AND COMPANY NAME | 6 |
| SPACE BETWEEN PARAGRAPHS | 4 | A TOTAL OF COUNTABLE UNITS (E.G. GLASSES OF WATER) | THE PROBLEM YOU ARE WRITING ABOUT | WRITER'S NAME AND JOB TITLE |
| FULLY BLOCKED STYLE | PRESENT TENSE | PLAIN ENGLISH | 5 | SALUTATION |
| PAST TENSE | DEFINE THE PURPOSE, THE PROBLEM AND THE READER | YOUR MAIN MESSAGE | OFFER ALTERNATIVES /MAKE HELPFUL SUGGESTIONS | 5 |
| FIND A LOGICAL ORDER FOR INFORMATION | USING APPROPRIATE LEVEL OF COURTESY IN WRITING | DECIDE WHAT YOU WANT TO SAY | 4 | PREPARE AN OUTLINE |

# CONCENTRATION

| DEFINITION | TERM | DEFINITION | TERM | DEFINITION |
| TERM | DEFINITION | TERM | DEFINITION | TERM |
| DEFINITION | TERM | DEFINITION | TERM | DEFINITION |
| TERM | DEFINITION | TERM | DEFINITION | TERM |

# INDEX

LaVergne, TN USA
17 March 2011
220550LV00001B/56/P